SAVING LAKES

The Urban Socio-Cultural and
Technological Perspectives

SAVING LAKES
The Urban Socio-Cultural and Technological Perspectives

Wun Jern Ng
NEWRI, NTU, Singapore

Sreeja Nair
NTU, Singapore

K B S N Jinadasa
University of Peradeniya, Sri Lanka

Evelyn Valencia
NEWRI, NTU, Singapore

World Scientific

EW JERSEY · LONDON · SINGAPORE · BEIJING · SHANGHAI · HONG KONG · TAIPEI · CHENNAI · TOKYO

Published by

World Scientific Publishing Co. Pte. Ltd.
5 Toh Tuck Link, Singapore 596224
USA office: 27 Warren Street, Suite 401-402, Hackensack, NJ 07601
UK office: 57 Shelton Street, Covent Garden, London WC2H 9HE

British Library Cataloguing-in-Publication Data
A catalogue record for this book is available from the British Library.

SAVING LAKES
The Urban Socio-Cultural and Technological Perspectives

Copyright © 2018 by World Scientific Publishing Co. Pte. Ltd.

ISBN 978-981-3271-25-8
ISBN 978-981-3272-46-0 (pbk)

For any available supplementary material, please visit
http://www.worldscientific.com/worldscibooks/10.1142/11014#t=suppl

Desk Editor: Amanda Yun

Typeset by Stallion Press
Email: enquiries@stallionpress.com

CONTENTS

PREFACE

Efforts towards protecting and restoring urban lakes have received increasing attention worldwide. Such lakes can be natural or man-made and provide a variety of ecosystem services. The latter includes their utility as a drinking water source, biodiversity spot and a mode of transport, apart from the aesthetic, cultural and recreational values they offer. Notwithstanding these values, many urban lakes are neglected and become dumping grounds for urban wastes as cities struggle for space and with waste disposal as populations and economies grow.

How is an urban lake important in the evolving city context and what is the role of the residents and civil society at large for its protection and appropriate use? Ornamental lakes are a delight to the public when they are clean, but who owns the lake when it deteriorates? The appeal for integrating social and cultural aspects in protection and pollution management of water bodies has been prevalent for a long time, but how exactly is this done? Once done, how is it sustained and the learning replicated in similar settings elsewhere? These were the questions the authors pondered on as an approach towards tropical urban lake remediation was designed and applied to the Kandy Lake located in the heart of the heritage city, Kandy in Sri Lanka.

Through this book the authors have attempted to bring out the duality of protecting culturally significant lakes; a situation where high cultural significance mandates their protection, but also limits the options available or permissible to be undertaken. This book documents the design of solutions to mitigate pollution in the Kandy Lake and Mid-Canal which drains from it. In the process it aims to serve as a reflection of the key factors that has led to the project's success, the road ahead and beginning of the project's expansion to other lakes in Sri Lanka. The approach in Kandy Lake was three-pronged; first, to improve the water quality in the lake via installation of floating wetlands and inflow management; second, through source control via wastewater treatment; and third, through awareness building via school education and capacity building of local engineers and contractors.

The authors hope that this book will serve as useful resource material to practitioners, students of civil and environmental engineering, water resources management, and social and environmental sciences, local communities, donors and research institutes towards understanding lake pollution as not only a technical issue, but also one that is rooted in the region's sociocultural history. The discussion in this book is based on work on Kandy Lake remediation that started in 2010 by a team of researchers based at the University of Peradeniya, Sri Lanka and Nanyang Technological University, Singapore and intends to demonstrate an example of taking a sociocultural lens to address the issue of lake pollution. The authors believe that some of the learning from the project can be adapted and transferred to other lakes in Sri Lanka and beyond. Though Kandy Lake, located next to the iconic Buddhist Temple Sri Dalada Maligawa that houses the Sacred Tooth Relic, is uniquely placed in terms of it being a symbol of national pride, without the concerted efforts of several actors and customisation of technological solutions to suit the sociocultural context, the lake may have suffered a fate similar to other polluted lakes across the world.

ABOUT THE AUTHORS

Ng Wun Jern was Director of Nanyang Environment & Water Research Institute (NEWRI) till July 2017, and lead Professor of the Environmental Bioinnovations Group (EBiG) at Nanyang Technological University (NTU), Singapore.

Prof. Ng interacts with the industry as an advisor in water and effluent treatment, and waterbody and soil remediation—and has brought numerous IPs to full-scale applications. Commercialised IPs include biosystems (e.g., aerobic [aeSBR], anaerobic [anSBR], anaerobic filter Anfil and pulsed bed [APBF] and hybrid anaerobic reactor Hybridan), materials, and equipment. His designs have been applied to some 140 full-scale installations in ASEAN, China, India, Sri Lanka and Taiwan. He has also founded spin-off companies, and was chairman of a major consulting company, senior advisor to listed companies and had served on the Singapore national water reclamation expert panel. He was a founding member of the Singapore Engineering Accreditation Board and was Vice-Dean at the Faculty of Engineering, National University of Singapore, and then Dean until 2003. In 2005, he was Singapore director of the Singapore-MIT Alliance serving the alliance universities — National University of Singapore, NTU and Massachusetts Institute of Technology till 2006. Thereafter, he was Director of Capability Development in the Environment & Water Industry Development Council at the Ministry of the Environment & Water Resources, working on national funding for research and development (R&D) and manpower development. In 2007, he joined NTU and became founding Executive Director at the NEWRI.

His research output may be found in some 600 publications which include journal papers, conference presentations, book chapters and monographs, reports, trade secrets and patents.

Prof. Ng's contributions to industry, research and education have been recognised with the ASEAN Engineering Award, Outstanding University Researcher Award, the Chevalier dans l'Ordre des Palmes

Academiques and the Tan Chin Tuan Centennial Professorship. In July 2017, a project he led was recognised with the IES Prestigious Project Award and thereafter, the ASEAN outstanding engineering award. He was also awarded the 2017 Singapore Energy Award, and the President's Technology Award for his work in the field of environmental engineering and wastewater management. In 2018, he was recognised as among the leading 100 scientists in Asia in the Asia Scientist 100 (2018 edition).

Sreeja Nair is a Postdoctoral Research Fellow at the School of Social Sciences, NTU, Singapore. She holds a PhD in Public Policy (Lee Kuan Yew School of Public Policy, National University of Singapore), and two Masters degrees: one in Climate and Society (Columbia University, USA) and the second in Environmental Studies (TERI University, India). Her research interests include environmental policy design under uncertainty and impacts of environmental change on communities, focusing on water and agriculture, particularly in South Asia. Her doctoral dissertation focused on cases from Indian agriculture to study the design and process of policy experimentation and piloting. She is currently associated with Nanyang Environment and Water Research Institute, NTU where she focuses on the sociopolitical dimensions of water sustainability projects and policy innovations in Asia. She is also an Instructor at the Public Policy and Global Affairs programme, NTU where she teaches Environmental Change and Policy Design.

Prior to joining her PhD, Dr Nair worked with the Energy and Resources Institute in India for seven years and contributed to diverse policy projects including the National Action Plan on Climate Change, state level Action Plans on Climate Change and scientific assessments of climate change impacts on local communities. She was also a contributing author for the Intergovernmental Panel on Climate Change's Fifth Assessment Report.

Shameen Jinadasa is a Senior Lecturer at the Department of Civil Engineering of the University of Peradeniya, Sri Lanka. Dr. Shameen has more than 20 years of water and wastewater related design experience, of which the last 10 years were in academia, research and consultancy.

He has been part of several research and development programmes both regionally and globally, applying his knowledge of Environmental Engineering designs and consultancy. He earned his BSc Eng in Civil Engineering from the University of Peradeniya, and MEng degree Singapore in Civil Engineering from the National University of Singapore. Subsequently, he obtained his PhD from Saitama University, Japan in 2006. Dr Jinadasa's area of expertise is environmental engineering with a special focus on developing sustainable water and wastewater management technologies for tropical developing countries. Dr Jinadasa has extensive experience coordinating international research projects on tropical constructed wetlands and coastal vegetation for tsunami protection in collaboration with researchers from Singapore, Japan, Australia, New Zealand and Sri Lanka.

Valencia Evelyn is Assistant Manager for NEWRI Community Development, at the NEWRI, NTU, Singapore. Ms Evelyn works with NEWRI Comm's project coordinators in Sri Lanka, Indonesia and Myanmar to plan, develop and manage their projects. Before joining the Lien Environmental Fellowship team full-time, in her final undergraduate years, she helped to conceptualise the environmental education programme piloted at the Mahamaya Girls' College for the LEF project 'Mitigation of Pollution in Kandy Lake and Mid-Canal, Sri Lanka'. She has a BEng in Environmental Engineering from NTU, Singapore, with exposure to humanities and arts subjects, including business law, communication studies, linguistics and literature.

ACKNOWLEDGEMENTS

The authors express their gratitude to a number of people for their contributions to this book and the project 'Mitigation of Pollution in Kandy Lake and Mid-Canal, Sri Lanka' that was the motivation behind developing this book. This book has immensely benefitted from the insights and anecdotes shared by several officials from the Kandy Water Board, Department of Irrigation and Kandy Municipal Council during and after the project. Specifically, we would like to acknowledge Dr. S.K. Weragoda, Mr. L.L.A. Peiris, Mr. N.I. Wickramasinghe, Mrs S.K.I. Wijewardena, Ms Chandani Devendra, Ms K.A.D. Kumudini, Ms Prabha Dassanayake, Mr Samadhi Wijekoon and Mr. H.A. Sunil Shantakumara for their contributions to the project and for lending their thoughts as quotes that are embedded throughout this book.

The collaboration between University of Peradeniya (UOP), Sri Lanka and Nanyang Technological University (NTU), Singapore was strengthened by members of the research and leadership team on both sides. Specifically the authors wish to register their thanks to the Vice Chancellor and former Vice Chancellors, Dean and former Deans of the Faculty of Engineering, Dr. G.B.B. Herath, Dr. C.S. Kalpage and their students, Dr. D.K. Jayarathne from the Department of Archaeology, UOP Professors, researchers and students at NTU and the Nanyang Environment and Water Research Institute (NEWRI).

This book has immensely benefitted from interviews with the Kandy community members as well as other prominent stakeholders of Kandy Lake including the Sri Dalada Maligawa, Mahamaya Girls College and contractors selected for implementing various technical activities under the project. Specifically, the authors would like to acknowledge the contributions of Mr. M.G. Gunarathne, Mr. Suranga Manohara, Mr. Dananjaya Kuruppu and Mr. Anura Bandara.

The authors thank the editorial team at World Scientific—specifically, Ms. Amanda Yun and Dr. Ng Han Yong—for their professional input on the manuscript. Finally, a word of appreciation goes to the Lien Foundation, without whose funding the Kandy project would not have been possible.

The list of contributors to the book as well as the project has been appended below.

Project contributors

Team at NTU, UOP, Water Board, Irrigation Department, Agelta, Enviromec.

Book contributors

Chapters 2 and 3 of the book have been written with significant contributions from Prof. Mallika Pinnawala and Prof. M.I.M. Mowjood, UOP. A special dedication goes to the late Prof. Shantha K. Hennayake, UOP for his critical insights on Kandy city and Kandy Lake.

CHAPTER 1

INTRODUCTION

1.1 Urban Lakes as a Socio-Cultural Complex

"Cities are not just brick and mortar; they represent the dreams, aspirations, and hopes of societies."

UN Habitat (2008)

Urban waterbodies such as lakes are intricately bound with a city's social fabric, and sociocultural aspects form a vital part of water resource management in urban areas (UNEP, 2000). Urban architecture and the lifestyle of its residents, for example, are two key cultural features that influence water resource management in cities and urban lakes (Marsalek et al., 2006). Urban lakes are valued for several reasons, including their utility as a drinking water reservoir, for ground water recharge, transportation, recreation and environmental value apart from aesthetic, historical and cultural significance (UNEP, 1994; Snehal and Unnati, 2012). Many urban lakes in Asia are seen to lose their original function for which these were constructed, often as a drinking and irrigation water source, due to declining water quality (Nagendra and Ostrom, 2014; Kora et al., 2017). Polluted water bodies gradually also lose their connection with traditional and potential future users, in turn impacting efforts towards their protection and remediation (Unnikrishnan et al., 2016).

The development and expansion of cities often occurs at crossroads between economic growth priorities and environmental and natural

1

resource management goals (DfID, 2010; Leichenko, 2011). The catchment area of urban lakes is often characterised by the presence of more impervious cover including roads, pavements and buildings (Schuler and Simpson, 2001; Henny and Meutia, 2014). The proximity of urban commercial and residential property to waterbodies can influence their prices and rentals depending on the aesthetic appeal and maintenance of these waterbodies. It is ironical that while development often leads to environmental degradation in cities, the presence of green spaces can lend themselves to projecting a city as being more liveable (Kauko et al., 2009; Rouwendal et al., 2017). However, in spite of their unique spatial, sociocultural and economic value and relationship with the city, urban lakes often end up as receptacles for wastes, or are infilled for development (Nazrul Islam et al., 2012; Nagendra and Ostrom, 2014).

Human civilisation has essentially thrived around water bodies (Gunawardhana et al., 2009; Mithen, 2010). In rural areas typically, waterbodies such as lakes also form points of social gathering and interaction. The links between the lake and the city are perhaps more pronounced and easily seen in rural compared to urban areas, and especially when rapid development changes a city's fabric. Unlike rural waterbodies where water is extracted for various purposes from rivers and lakes, similar commonly accessible water supply sources have become redundant in many urban spaces over time. Many cities instead are found to maintain lakes and rivers for leisure and aesthetic purposes (Anderson and Tabb, 2002). Another difference between waterbodies in rural and urban areas is that in rural areas, the lake or reservoir may not have an alternative in terms of the functions it provides, but in urban areas there may be an alternate drinking water supply, making the lake lose its direct relevance in the people's daily life. Conservation of the natural functions of an urban lake necessitates lake management strategies that are localised or context-driven in their approach in order to be sustained over time.[1] However urban lakes and reservoirs, in the context of the cityscape, may not be in direct view of people and so they may not be aware that they are adversely affecting it.

Many of these urban lakes have an evolving relationship with the city they are associated with and hold their importance in terms of providing

---

[1] http://www.mdpi.com/2073-4441/9/4/233/htm#B4-water-09-00233.

a sense of 'collective identity, community and belonging' to communities living in close proximity to the lake, and citizens at large (Strang, 2012). Typically, lakes in rapidly urbanising regions share several characteristics. These include facing influx of untreated solid wastes and wastewater from nearby establishments, including settlements, peri-urban agricultural fields and sometimes industries, high runoff volumes during rains, being encroached on and infilled for development of real estate, serving as tourist attractions, facing seasonal algal blooms with attendant water quality and aesthetic deterioration, facing changes in aquatic life quality and numbers—including occasional fish mortality, high pollutant concentration observed during the dry season, and presence of multiple stakeholders in its management.

An urban lake typically 'belongs' to multiple stakeholders who derive value from the lake, including the city's residents and visitors. The wellbeing of the urban population, which in turn is dependent on environmental factors such as the quality of air, land, and water is further influenced by urban governance, land management, legislation, financing, and cooperation between multiple stakeholders (SIDA, 2007). Policy efforts towards building resilience to urban environmental pollution is challenged by mismatch between the timescale over which urban planners operate (few decades) and the timescale over which the impact of policy decisions related to the urban environment are likely to be observed (ranging from decades to a century; Bai et al., 2010; Fig. 1.1). This mismatch makes it all the more imperative that remediation of urban environmental issues such as lake pollution is done judiciously—that is, while balancing developmental priorities and trade-offs for the environment and considering minimisation of environmental damages as some of these may be irreversible and more expensive to rectify in the future.

This book documents the evolution of pollution mitigation efforts in Kandy Lake, Sri Lanka. Kandy is a UNESCO world heritage city and the Kandy Lake has high social, cultural and political significance due to its long-standing history and its location next to the sacred Buddhist Temple of the Tooth (Sri Dalada Maligawa). While technologies to manage lake pollution are well-researched, appropriate, targeted and concerted efforts are required to apply proven technologies, sensitive to the context in order for these to be sustainable and suitable to be handed over to the local authorities

Temporal scale of planning

(a)

Urban land use planning

Urban infrastructure development

Industrial development strategy

Purchase of utility goods

Transportation planning

Solid waste management

Public service pricing

0   5   10   15   20   25

Years

Temporal scale of environmental implications
of decisions

(b)

Urban land use planning

Urban infrastructure development

Industrial development strategy

Purchase of utility goods

Transportation planning

Solid waste management

Public service pricing

1   10   100   1000

Years

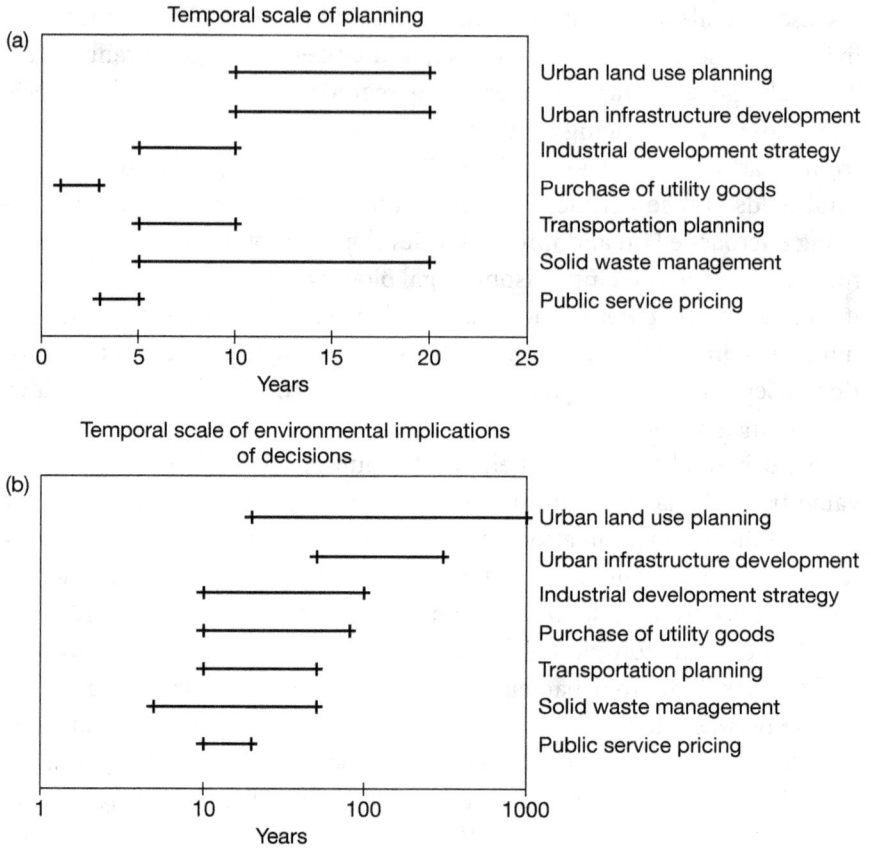

Fig 1.1 Timescales of urban decision making: (a) temporal scale of urban planning and (b) temporal scale of environmental implications of policy decisions. Source: Bai et al. (2010).

and communities for long-term management. In Sri Lanka, urban lakes have been built for different purposes over time such as for drinking water provision, irrigation and aesthetic value (Fig. 1.2).

Kandy city is located 500 m above sea level and is the second largest city in Sri Lanka, housing more than 100,000 residents and a large number of floating population, up to six times higher than the permanent residents. Kandy is also Sri Lanka's heritage capital, where the last kingdom of Sri Lanka was. Kandy has rightly been called the city of living heritage as it bears witness to over 600 years of recorded local history. Since the

Fig 1.2 Lakes in Sri Lanka and their different purposes (from top left to bottom right: Kurunegala Lake as a drinking water source, Gregory Lake for tourism and irrigation, Kandy Lake for aesthetic and cultural value; Thissa wewa, Anuradhapura for drinking and informally used for bathing).

colonial time, three generations of kings ruled the Kingdom of Sri Lanka from Kandy. The Buddhist monasteries, Asgiriya and Malwatta, were also established in Kandy in 1753. From 1592 onwards Kandy was the last remaining independent kingdom on the island since the coastal regions had then been conquered by the Portuguese (SCDP, 2014).

While Kandy Lake's political and cultural prominence were strong factors to mandate its protection; this also limited the bundle of options feasible (or acceptable) for implementation towards pollution mitigation. This book focuses on characterising this dilemma and drawing lessons from on-ground experience in designing solutions for Kandy Lake that were not only technically-sound, but also in line with the sociocultural and political sensitivities and engagement of key stakeholders within the design process to ensure acceptance of the efforts and sustainability of the solution implemented.

1.2   Challenges for Urban Lakes in Tropical Settings

Many tropical lakes in Asian urban centres are facing the brunt of years of unplanned urbanisation, which in turn affects provision of public services including wastewater collection, treatment and disposal. Sometimes this is attributed to limited financial and technical capacities in these regions. In recent years, there has been an increased focus on development of high rate and increasingly compact sanitation systems that require high energy inputs, installation and operational costs, and technical expertise for their operation and maintenance. Apart from their high costs, these may not be sustainable owing to their large carbon footprint (Manatunge and Witharana, 2011). The development of low-cost yet effective urban sanitation measures suited to context is thus a continuing challenge.

The nature of pollutants entering an urban waterbody can differ based on the extent of urbanisation and industrialisation. These could include oils, gasoline and additives, fertilizer and pesticide run-off from agricultural fields, chemicals and industrial wastes and domestic wastes. These pollutants can be discharged directly or indirectly into adjacent waterbodies without adequate treatment to remove harmful compounds. Water pollution reduces the availability of oxygen in the waterbody, and eventually the fish and plankton become susceptible to the alterations these pollutants induce in water. Pollution affects the chemistry of water, and this can mean changes in the temperature, texture and pH, among other parameters, of the original condition. This can further threaten the flora and fauna of the lake ecosystem. Treatment at source is important because once these pollutants, for example, heavy metals, enter the waterbodies it is much more difficult and costlier to remediate then.

Tropical lakes such as Kandy typically have uniformly high temperatures throughout the year, further enhancing plant growth dynamics and microbial kinetics compared to those in temperate regions (Tanaka and Weragoda, 2011). Tropical lakes, however, still do show seasonal variations in primary production (biological productivity) and subsequent decay and decline in oxygen levels, usually following heavy runoff during the rainy season when nutrients and organic matter are washed into the lakes (Dinar et al., 1995).

In the last few decades, the city has grown substantially with commerce and tourism. People from outside the city come to Kandy for business, education, medical treatment, tourism and religious pilgrimages. Kandy Lake is part of the Mahaweli River catchment which supplies water to large parts of Sri Lanka. As the city grows, so does its solid wastes and wastewater loads. Kandy city generates wastewater volumes of about 20,000 m³ per day. There are many hotels, nursing homes, schools and illegal squatter settlements around the Kandy Lake and so a large amount of wastewater is generated, which eventually finds its way to the lake and Mid-Canal, untreated (NWSDB, 2016). Downstream at the Mahaweli River, there are water intake points for the drinking water supply to Kandy and thus polluting Kandy Lake holds a potential public health hazard.

Between 1999 and 2009, there were severe algal bloom episodes at Kandy Lake resulting in fish deaths. While local authorities and experts acknowledged the need for integrated water and catchment management, they were faced with several challenges that impeded any remedial action in Kandy. These included having limited resources such as space scarcity with limitations to expansion as the city is surrounded by hills, cost and selection of appropriate wastewater treatment technology, the need to preserve the natural and historical landscape of Kandy city, and the need for public participation to keep the lake clean.

A number of solutions have been tried in the past for Kandy Lake pollution management but none of these have worked as a 'solve-all' to mitigate the lake's pollution. It was in this context that the project 'Mitigation of Pollution in Kandy Lake and Mid-Canal' was started by a group of researchers at the University of Peradeniya, Sri Lanka and Nanyang Technological University, Singapore, with support from the Lien Foundation. Lessons from the Kandy Lake pollution remediation project, which forms the focus of this book, are currently being expanded to Kurunegala Lake. Kurunegala Lake, in contrast to Kandy Lake, is a source of drinking water, much bigger and with a different topography but still requiring remediation efforts in terms of pollution management and lake clean-up.

1.3   Overview of the Book

This book documents the process of innovation and implementation of solutions for protection and pollution management in an urban lake in a tropical setting, and the need and motivation behind the design of solutions. It explores design requirements based on the need for sensitivity to religious and cultural norms, social values, and aesthetic requirements. First-hand experiences of the authors in planning and implementing a lake remediation project in Kandy city, the heritage capital of Sri Lanka, have been drawn upon to provide practical examples of the issues. Although Kandy is a unique case, the learning from the lake remediation efforts and approach can be adapted to other lakes in Sri Lanka and elsewhere in tropical regions while allowing for the fact that each lake has its history woven into its catchment's social fabric. The latter would then require conscious, concerted and sustained action to engage citizens in the management of their resources. The authors argue it is essential to tie technological solutions to the sociocultural aspects of the region. This understanding is far from being easy to achieve and implement in practice, and this book documents the authors' experience at doing so, the learning in terms of the consequent challenges, and opportunities to take the efforts further and to replicate these with appropriate modification. The authors believe this book is the first of its kind, discussing the practice and challenges in implementing such projects, in a sensitive context in terms of the location's strategic prominence and high sociocultural, historical and political significance. The latter, many-a-times, had even superseded the technical and economic requirements in terms of importance.

This book highlights the integrated efforts towards lake management, including construction of a sewage treatment plant (STP) within the premises of the Tooth Relic temple—Sri Dalada Maligawa adjoining the Kandy Lake, floating wetlands introduced in the Kandy Lake and set-up of the Wetlands Education Centre at Mahamaya Girls' College—a premier educational institution in Kandy. The project efforts led to new initiatives for pollution management including silt trap construction and rehabilitation of Mid-Canal with the support of international donor agencies such as Japan International Cooperation Agency and the World Bank. Local authorities in Kandy continued their efforts to keep Kandy Lake and Kandy city clean. The Irrigation Department of Kandy continues to maintain the wetlands, and has set up new fencing and signboards to protect Kandy Lake following the clean-up. Fish feeding and littering into the lake have reduced noticeably. The Kandy Water Board is now in the process of constructing sewerage lines and a wastewater treatment plant for Kandy.

The project planning and implementation itself was an evolutionary process. Knowing the complexity of the urban setting of Kandy, it was understood that the approach would essentially need to be organic with the idea of 'learning as we go' allowing scope for it to be adapted as the project went along, without losing sight of the overall objective. The book particularly captures the sociocultural and political dimensions of lake water management, with the hope that it becomes an example of integrated efforts in water sustainability. The book chapters have been developed by the combined team of researchers with inputs from various stakeholders in Kandy city and Colombo. The latter were interviewed during and after project implementation. The interviewees included officials from various government departments and research institutes in Sri Lanka, and communities living around Kandy Lake. Secondary literature on Kandy city and lake and on pollution management efforts in other urban lakes with similar settings was also consulted.

A highlight of this book is the various quotes that have been drawn out from the interviews. These provided several anecdotes from history and personal experiences from Kandy residents as well as practitioners and researchers having worked for several years and decades on issues related to Kandy Lake and its pollution. These quotes have been positioned in the book to provide a sense of immediacy to the project and to validate our observations as well as literature. These serve to enrich the arguments in the book while providing a range of perspectives and ideas regarding urban lake protection and management from the community's level.

The authors expect this book to be of interest to a multi-disciplinary audience, primarily as the book has benefited from inputs from persons from a variety of academic backgrounds as well as professional affiliations including engineers (civil, environmental), sociologists, political scientists, water policy practitioners and the common citizen. The contents of the book are spread across six chapters. All chapters drew on the experiences from the Kandy project to drive the example, and add empirics to the concepts. Chapter 2 starts with tracing the dual relationship between an urban lake and the city and how one influences the other in a symbiotic way. The chapter then discusses the history and evolution of Kandy city and its relation to the lake's development. Chapter 3 identifies the major stakeholders around the problem and challenges of stakeholder engagement. Chapter 4 presents how changing socio-economic and environmental context affects urban lakes and how the issue of pollution came about in Kandy city and Lake. Chapter 5 elaborates the approach and development of solutions for Kandy Lake pollution management and how these were adopted. In conclusion, Chapter 6 presents the overall learning from the lake pollution management efforts and discusses opportunities and challenges for its adoption, and replication with modification.

CHAPTER 2

LAKE AND THE CITY: INTER-RELATIONSHIPS

Kandy Lake is part of the Sri Lankan identity.

Dr. S.K. Weragoda, National Water Supply and Drainage Board, Kandy

The (Kandy) Lake is an organic component of Kandy. It is difficult to think of Kandy without the Lake. This was the same thinking decades back and even now . . .

Late Prof. S.K. Hennayake, UOP

This chapter highlights how the interrelationships between an urban lake and the city are influenced by its physical characteristics including its geographical location and morphology as well as its history. Using the case of Kandy Lake, the chapter highlights how the geographical placement of an urban lake and its history influences its condition over time in terms of its utility, quality and overall importance. These factors further influence the socio-economic value and political, cultural and environmental significance of the lake in the present date.

2.1 Influence of Physical Characteristics

The city of Kandy is located 500 m above sea level. To its north, the lake is flanked by two places of significance, the Royal Palace and the Temple of the Tooth, known as the Dalada Maligawa. Kandy Lake spans over an area of 0.18 km² with a maximum depth of 13 m (Silva, 2003). Kandy is surrounded by a triangular mountain range—the Hantana and Knuckles mountain ranges. The entrances to the city are located at the apex of the triangle and towards the valley on the eastern mountain range. Construction on the hilly slopes of the city has made it prone to landslides and earth slips during heavy rains. The mean annual rainfall during the monsoon period (April–August) is 1,800–2,500 mm (SCDP, 2014).

The built area of Kandy has been developed around the quadrangular Kandy Lake in a somewhat rectangular layout. The northern edge of the city holds the administrative buildings of the old capital, including the Kandy Municipal Council (KMC). This part of the city is densely populated (Fig. 2.1) along a grid of streets, commercial buildings and designated historic buildings. Many of these streets and infrastructure, including storm water drainage, were built during the colonial times but are still functional (SCDP, 2014).

There are five major inlets (Fig. 2.2) and 29 minor drains entering the lake. Figure 2.1 shows the five major inlets. They are 1. *Hillwood* Inflow, 2. *Saranankara* Inflow, 3. *Mahamaya* Inflow, 4. *Rathu Bokkuwa* Inflow and 5. *B.P.T.* Inflow. The 29 other natural and artificial streams discharge into lake during the rainy season. There is a spillway at the downstream end of the lake (opposite the 'Sri Dalada Maligawa'), and is the only outlet and is controlled with a sluice gate used during the two peak rainy seasons (April–May/October–December) (Jinadasa et al., 2011).

Fig 2.1 Glimpses of the busy Kandy city.

Fig 2.2 Kandy Lake and its main inlets.

The lake has two morphologically distinct basins; about 75% of the basin has a depth of 4 m and the rest has a depth of over 10 m (Silva, 2007). Oxygen depletion at the bottom of Kandy Lake has been reported (due to stratification) and is indicative of the organic matter accumulation in the bottom sediments (Abel, 1989). Kandy Lake is a relatively stagnant waterbody with a deep part where the water column is not well mixed. Under such conditions, when organic matter trapped among the sediments over time decays, it can lead to formation of anoxic conditions (less dissolved oxygen), especially in the dead zones which may lead to fish deaths.

Despite its key location and function in Kandy city's cultural life and tourist economy, unregulated urbanisation and the lack of adequate waste disposal and management facilities has resulted in serious pollution of the lake waters due to discharge of waste into waterways feeding the lake. A canal (called Mid-Canal or 'Meda Ela') originates from the overflow sluice of Kandy Lake, and runs through the densely populated city before draining into the Mahaweli River (Fig. 2.3).

The Mahaweli is the main source of water for Kandy city and one of the largest water intakes is just a few hundred meters downstream of the discharge point of the Mid-Canal (Abeygunawardane et al., 2011). This canal receives wastewater from several washing places, laundries and Batik cloth

Fig 2.3 Kandy Lake as part of the Mahaweli River catchment.

Fig 2.4 A section of the polluted Mid-Canal.

dyeing operations, as well as discharges of diesel and other automobile waste liquids from garages and workshops. Topographically, being situated at a lower elevation, a large number of side canals also discharge into the Mid-Canal (Figs 2.4 and 2.5). The canal is approximately 10–15 m in width and is covered only in parts. It is otherwise an open channel and hence receives a large load of waste matter, particularly during the rainy seasons. A large number of houses are situated along the canal and some of these dwellers depend on unprotected wells close to the canal for water for their drinking and domestic uses. In most cases, only a thin soil cover separates the canal from the wells. For the most part of its course, the canal runs on a crystalline limestone bed. A sustainable water quality improvement plan to mitigate the pollution in Kandy Lake and Mid-Canal would thus essentially need to be systematic and integrated as the pollution in both systems are interrelated and ultimately impacting the Mahaweli.

Fig 2.5 Outlet structure at Kandy Lake where it discharges to the Mid-Canal.

2.2   History Matters

'Kandy Lake and the Temple of the Tooth are connected both physically, and spiritually'

Mr. W.M.G.A. Bandara, Temple Secretary, Sri Dalada Maligawa

'After the 1980s, pollution from upstream was very bad; with 190 hotels in operation'.

Dr S.K. Weragoda, NWSDB

'In the 1970s, Sri Lanka opened its economy. One of the benefits of this is that Kandy became a tourist centre, but the downside is environmental damage'.

Late Prof. S.K. Hennayake, UOP

Several large, medium and small reservoirs including lakes have been constructed by kings in Sri Lanka to meet the water demand for agriculture and other human activities in response to the inadequacy of rainfall and its poor distribution in the dry season in most parts of the country along with the excess of evaporation and transpiration, resulting in frequent droughts and consequent crop loss (Amarasiri, 2015).

In 1865, a Dutch architect drew a map of Kandy showing five tanks. The first one was *Bogambara Wawa* (also called lower Lake) built by *Wemaladharamasuriya* situated in a paddy field. In 1887, the lower lake was filled up on the argument that space was required for urban expansion, expenses related to desilting, and spread of malaria and waterborne diseases in the area. Today this place is used as a sports recreation ground. The second tank called *Borawewa* was established in 1832 between two schools, the Trinity and Vidyartaha. The third called *Udawattha Wawa* or Royal Lake was constructed by King Rajasinhae II. The fourth tank was called *Mawilmada Wawa* and the last, Kandy Lake, was then called *Kiri Muhudha* (Sea of Milk) since it was constructed with clay which was white in colour. It was established between 1807 and 1812 by King Sri Wicrama Rajasingha (Silva, 2003).

Kandy Lake is flanked by the Hanthana–Mattanpathana range of mountains on one side and the Udawathhakale range of mountains on the other and continues into the Bogambara Wawa. The exit from this Wawa is the Meda Ela which then discharges into the Mahaweli River. It is said the king had used land that was previously a paddy field to construct the lake.

The lake has two main features. One is the island in the middle of the lake and the other is the Walakulu Bemma (Cloud Wall or Cloud Drift Wall). Construction was first done by removing earth from both the palace end and the Malwatte Vihare end, leaving an island. At first, this island was used as the Royal Summer House for the Queen and the ladies of the court to relax. It was called Diyathilake Mandapaya but the British had subsequently used it as an ammunition store and added a fortress-style parapet around its boundary. The Cloud Wall (Fig. 2.6) surrounding the lake faces the built-up area of the city and was completed by the British as King Sri Wickrama Rajasinghe had been unable to complete the wall before the

Fig 2.6 Ornamental Cloud Wall around the lake.

Fig 2.7 Queen's bath under renovation (as of November 2017).

city was captured by the British. The Ulpange (Queen's bath) (Fig. 2.7) also formed an important feature of the area's architecture (Silva, 1985).

Historical records suggest Kandy was first established by Vikramabahu III (1357–1374 CE), who ruled the Kingdom of Gampola. The city was then named Senkadagalapura. In 1592, Kandy became the capital city of the last remaining independent kingdom in Sri Lanka after the coastal regions had been conquered by the Portuguese. As the capital, Kandy also became home to the relic of the tooth of the Buddha a tradition that started in the fourth century making the Sinhalese monarch guardian of the relic and so symbolising the direct connection between the Buddhist religion and the right to rule the land. The Royal Palace and the Temple of the Tooth were placed in close proximity to each other. In 1815, with the surrender of the King of Kandy to the British, a treaty known as the Kandyan Convention was signed between the British and the Radalas (Kandyan aristocrats). With this treaty, Kandy recognised George III as its king and became a British protectorate. During the British period in Sri Lanka, the history of Kandy and its townscape witnessed rapid and significant change.

The main purpose of constructing the lake had been to meet the needs of the royal family and ordinary locals did not have any access to the lake then. After the Sinhalese Kingdom fell to the British, the ordinary people were allowed to use the lake. In recent history, 20% of the water requirement of the city had been supplied by the lake. This was stopped in 1989 and the pump house of the lake was converted into an office of a government agency. With population increase, the city including the lake gradually became polluted. It became the receiving end of many sewer lines, especially those from the temples adjoining the lake. There were nearly 128 drains discharging into Kandy Lake at one time (Karunaratna, 1999). With the increase of pollution many forms of aquatic life such as turtles began to disappear. As an ornamental lake to the Sri Dalada Maligawa today, no fishing, bathing or draw off for irrigation is permitted at the lake (Silva, 2007). Officially, the KMC prohibited washing and bathing in the lake due to public health concerns in 1873.

The problem of water pollution in Kandy Lake was an issue of concern even during the British period. A colonial doctor, Dickman noted rising pollution in the lake in 1861 due to waste that flowed into Kandy Lake from the Military Hospital and the KMC addressed the problem. In addition, during the period of coffee plantations in the country (before tea was introduced in Sri Lanka, coffee was the major commercial crop). The water used for pulping coffee from the Walker Estate and the Roseneath Estate nearby flowed into the lake and caused silting. The then governor Gregory built a retaining wall extending along the bend on the road near the land where Mahamaya Girls' College stands today to prevent the silting of the lake in 1873. This is now an ornamental pond and a silt trap.

During this period, silting of the lake was also a critical issue of concern. It was reported in 1878, that in order to prevent silting, the then-secretary of KMC suggested to the Colonial Secretary that the land on either side of the stream feeding the lake should be protected with plants and trees. It was permitted and MC purchased 9 acre of land from Roseneath Estate Store and grew plants and trees to protect the lake. But today these measures are not practiced and buildings, mainly for tourism related activities have been allowed to be constructed in the aforesaid areas. The resulting discharge to the lake had increased silting and authorities have had the added burden of desilting the lake at substantial cost. For example, in 1914 the cost for desilting was around 3,000 LKR and the task was sponsored by Walker and Sons Co. Ltd. and Ch Hustan and Co. of Colombo supplied the iron barges. In 1989, the lake was de-silted at a cost of 12 million LKR and all silt traps rebuilt and a drain was constructed from the Mahamaya college site up to the spillway along Sangaraja Mawatha to take the polluted water away. In addition, migrants who had worked as coolies had settled on government lands and railway and road reservations. One such place was the Mid-Canal that is now the most polluted area in Kandy since it is without proper infrastructure to support such settlements.

2.3   Valuing the Kandy Lake

'When danger threatened the land, the first concern of the monarch and the people going to war was the protection and safety of the Tooth Relic—considered the noblest and most meritorious duty in Sinhale. The Dalada symbolized the religion and equated with the love for motherland and all that the land symbolized—their harvests, homes, families, culture and way of life'

Nanayakkara (1971)

The relationship between an urban lake and its socio-economic components is prone to change over time, based on factors such as size of the lake, its location and distance to populated areas (Dinar et al., 1995). A number of factors make Kandy Lake invaluable to the city's residents and Sri Lankans in general. First, in the minds of the local people Kandy is still the capital of the hill country, rather the last indigenous capital of the country. Second, in the imagination of people, the Sri Dalada Maligawa is the centre of Buddhism in the world. Third, the weather in Kandy is pleasant and one of the factors making it so is the presence of the Kandy Lake, flanked by two forests in close proximity.

Kandy Lake is a popular spot for people in Kandy from all walks of life and all ages. It is not only a place of beauty for visitors to Kandy but also for locals, the young and the old to come and relax especially during the evenings. It is a common scene to see people strolling around the lake (Figs 2.8 and 2.9). Kandy Lake is also home to many types of flora and fauna (Fig. 2.10). A variety of trees that include Nuga, Palm, Sal, Mara and fruit trees have been planted along the lake, some of them being nearly a hundred years old. Common animal species seen at the lake include monitor lizards, frogs as well as birds such as the Indian Cormorant, White Egret Crane, Wood Stork and Pelican (MCDP, 2014).

Economic activities based on the lake can be divided into two categories. One is the activities that depend directly on the lake such as recreational

Fig 2.8 Scenes around Kandy Lake.

Fig 2.9 Child looking at the ducks in Kandy Lake.

activities conducted on commercial basis. The most visible of these is the boat service for local and foreign tourists but this is done on a small scale and often is not well organised. There is also an active informal economy around the lake providing livelihood to a large number of people in and around Kandy. This includes the vendors selling fruit, gram and drinks. There are also sellers of flowers to worshippers to the Temple of the Tooth nearby. Another group that depends on the visitors and users of the lake is itinerant in nature. These include the beggars and fortune tellers such as palm readers. The size of this informal economy however is difficult to ascertain. Hotels around Kandy Lake (Fig. 2.11) benefit economically from the Kandy Lake as the lake and the Dalada Maligawa draw numerous tourists annually.

Fig 2.10 Flora and fauna around Kandy Lake.

Fig 2.11 Queen's hotel (one of the first to start in the area).

A recent study (Hirayama et al., 2015) on community preferences for sustainable management of Kandy Lake reveals high importance is accorded to the lake as a spot of religious, cultural, historical and touristic relevance. The younger generation, however, emphasised recreational functions like swimming, boating and bird watching, more than the older generation.

The population of Kandy is around 120,000 with a floating population of 150,000 commuters daily. The city experiences a two- to three-fold population increase during the internationally renowned annual *Esela Perahara* (Kandy Procession) season in July–August (Fig. 2.12).

As mentioned earlier the lake had been closely connected to the Royal Family of the country and the Temple of the Tooth. According to Roberts Knox (1966), who described Kandy Lake as 'the small pond of Kandy', it had been connected with the Temple of the Tooth from the reign of King Rajasinhe II. There is evidence the religious and cultural significance of the lake has grown further today (Figs 2.13 and 2.14).

Further, the inner city and outer city concept was important to the Kandyan kingdom and Kandy Lake performed a significant role in this division. It also provided security and beauty to the Royal Palace as, according to the legends, there was a tunnel from Kandy Lake to the forest area adjoining the Temple of the Tooth called the *Udawattha Kele* (Forest) and this served as an emergency escape route for the king in the event of an overwhelming invasion and he had felt need to seek safety.

Kandy Lake given its association with a world heritage city and also for its association with the Temple of the Tooth has influence over political affairs as well. Any decision with regard to the lake requires the approval

Fig 2.12 Perahara festival.

Fig 2.13 Kandy Lake and the *Sri Dalada Maligawa.*

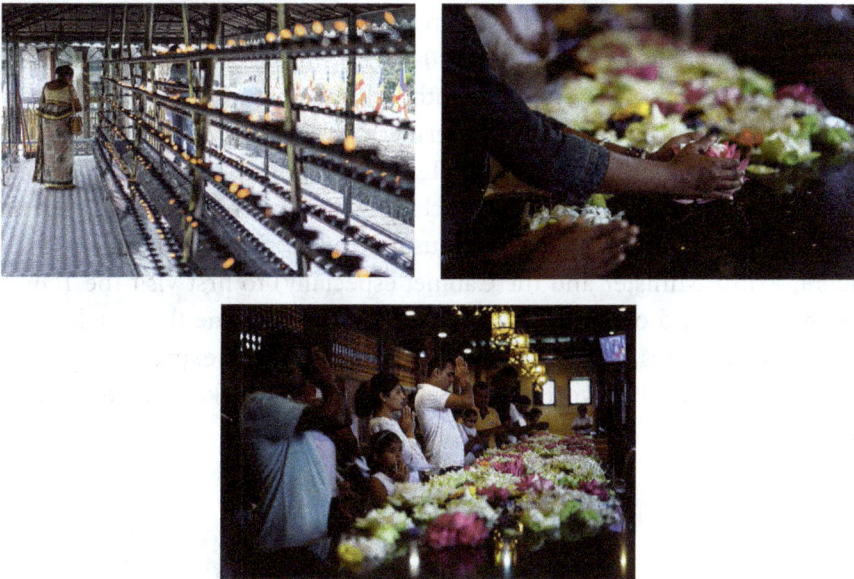

Fig 2.14 Devotees praying inside the temple.

of the *Mahanayakas*[1] though the administration is formally under the government and Municipal Council, the District Secretary and other related line ministries and provincial ministries are involved. For example, today it is identified that air pollution in Kandy city is drastically increasing, along with tyre waste runoff entering the lake owing to the slowly moving traffic along the lake. One of the reasons for this increase in the air pollution is

---

[1] Mahanayakas are high-ranked Buddhist monks.

the road closure to the main entrance of the Temple (following a terrorist attack in 1998). This created a longer detour around the Temple. The closure was initiated during the civil war but to date no decision has been made to change the arrangement for political reasons.

When Sri Lanka gained independence in 1948, Kandy was one of the several secondary level regional cities but as the seat of the Tooth Relic and for the fact that it was the capital of the last kingdom, Kandy had enjoyed a special status among them. Two important developments had subsequently further enhanced the standing of Kandy among cities in the country. First, is the emergence of Sinhalese Buddhists, who are over 70% of the country's population, as the decisive power in politics in the mid-1950s and crystallization of their power in the 1970s. With this development, Buddhism attained a special status and the Tooth Relic acquired the role of legitimising the country's rulers in the modern era. Everything associated with the Tooth Relic, the two main Buddhist Temples responsible for the Tooth Relic and the associated historical sites, including the lake, thus acquired a special status in the country. Today it is a must for the newly elected leaders (President, Prime Minister and the Cabinet especially) to first visit the Temple of the Tooth and obtain blessings. Nothing can be done that might affect the historical sites linked to Tooth Relic without the expressed approval and blessings of the two Head Priests, the Mahanayakas, responsible for the Temple of the Tooth.

CHAPTER 3

WHO 'OWNS' AN URBAN LAKE?

All stakeholders should be equal partners in the lake's conservation.

Prof. M.I.M. Mowjood, Faculty of Agriculture, UOP

This chapter discusses the dilemmas associated with managing multiple stakeholders and their incentives which affect the well-being of an urban lake. Acknowledgement of importance as a heritage site often does not equate to lake protection. It needs concerted efforts in principle but what makes it difficult in practice? 'The ownership'.

3.1   Management of an Urban Lake

Who owns an urban lake is a pertinent question to be asked as the connection of many urban lakes with their users (both traditional and current) grows weaker as these lakes get polluted. There are rather extreme examples of lakes being converted into facilities such as bus interchanges, stadiums and malls—purposes that are completely different from the original intended use of the lake space (Unnikrishnan et al., 2016).

The question 'who owns Kandy Lake' does not have a simple answer. From being a king's private tank, the Kandy Lake has witnessed changing ownership and thereby responsibility towards its protection and management. The lake has a complex network of stakeholders, as identified in Figures 3.1 and 3.2 who are linked to the lake in different ways, such as:

Fig 3.1 Who owns Kandy Lake?

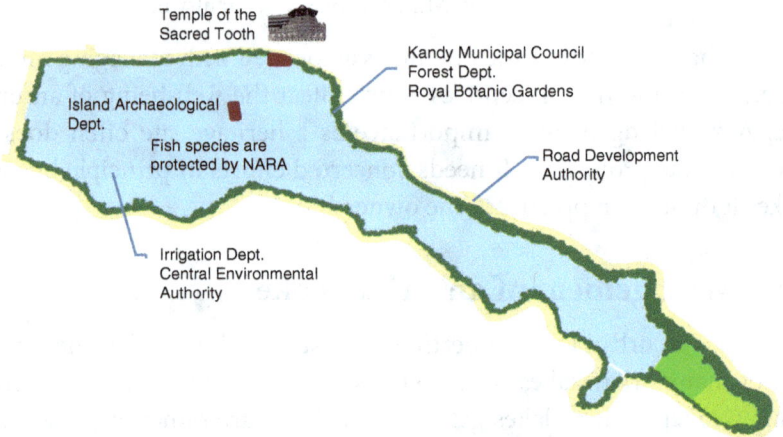

Fig 3.2 Network of stakeholders in and around Kandy Lake (compiled by authors through interviews). (NARA, National Aquatic Resources Research and Development Agency).

- Who is responsible for day-to-day management of activities in Kandy Lake? (Irrigation Department, Kandy Municipal Council [KMC])
- Who discharges wastewater into the Kandy Lake? (Restaurants, Residents, Schools)

- Who are adversely affected due to pollution? (Sri Dalada Maligawa, Public, Pilgrims, Tourists)
- Who sets standards, monitors and implements regulations? (Central Environmental Authority [CEA])
- Who funds the management? (Local bodies, Universities, Other institutions)
- Who has know-how on the subject of pollution management? (Universities and research institutions)
- Who are benefited by the services that the lake offers? (Public, Tourists, Ecosystem)
- Whose voice is not generally heard but affected? (Aquatic flora and fauna)

Table 3.1 highlights the functions, roles and responsibilities of key stakeholders in Kandy Lake pollution management and the challenges faced. A water body is an inclusive system, cannot be isolated and managed hence a multiple ownership model for lake management needs to be considered.

3.1.1   Sri Dalada Maligawa

The major draw of local and foreign tourists alike to Kandy is the Temple of the Tooth Relic. The Sri Dalada Maligawa is a world famous pilgrimage site. As the Kandy Lake is located in the middle of the historically important, sacred and heritage city, it plays an important role with respect to the aesthetic values, ecosystem and health and sanitation of the people.

3.1.2   Kandy Municipal Council

The KMC is governed by the Mayor, with members elected by the people and a Commissioner appointed by the government. The KMC comprises various departments responsible for maintaining different aspects of Kandy Lake. The departments of Health, Environment and Buildings play a major role in enforcing the policies and regulations related to Kandy Lake. Local government acts, municipal and urban councils' ordinances, the Pradeshiya Sabha act, Land Development Ordinances (No. 19 of 1935, No. 3 of 1946), the Land Acquisition Act, and the Crown Land Ordinance (No. 8 of 1947, 9 of 1947 and 13 of 1949) are prescribed in the government policy for land development and rehabilitation, and to maintain the reservation area.

Table 3.1 Key institutions, their roles and responsibilities and challenges in management of Kandy Lake and its surroundings.

Institutions	Role/Responsibilities	Challenges
Sri Dalada Maligawa	Keep the vicinity clean for pilgrims and visitors	Has little technical expertise for wastewater management
		Surge of visitors during festival days result in large variable of wastewater load from kitchens and toilets of the Maligawa
Kandy Municipal Council	Approval for construction of houses	Limited funds
		Illegal residents
	Maintaining infrastructure (roads, drainage etc.)	Solid waste disposal and collection in informal settlements
	Collection and disposal of solid wastes	Littering, especially from people coming from outside Kandy
Urban Development Authority	Approve new construction and town planning	Rapid increase in demand for infrastructure
		Lack of space for city expansion
Irrigation Department	Upkeep of the lake	No authority to create or impose laws to regulate upstream activities
		Limited funds
		No designated facility to monitor lake water quality
Public Health Sector	Health policy implementation	Lack of obvious direct link between polluted lake and public health

Institutions	Role/Responsibilities	Challenges
	Monitoring of effluent discharge	Large cost associated with conducting such study
	Responsible for public health and sanitation	Difficulty in dealing with public and government institutions in monitoring and implementation of regulations
	Public awareness	
	Legal actions	
Central Environmental Authority	Regulation of environmental discharges	Informal settlements
		Illegal dumping of wastewater at night
	Grant Environmental Protection Licence (EPL) for medium and large industries and processing plants	Unauthorised construction, sometimes due to political advantages
	Monitoring the effluent discharges	Difficulty in dealing with public and government institutions in monitoring and implementation of regulations
	Legal actions	
University of Peradeniya and Institute of Fundamental Studies	Human resource development	Typically, no authority to carry out large-scale implementation
	Research and development	Limited funds
	Monitoring: data collection, analysis, reporting/ publish scientific articles	
	New technology: development and dissemination	

(Continued)

Table 3.1 Key institutions, their roles and responsibilities and challenges in management of Kandy Lake and its surroundings. (*Continued*)

Institutions	Role/Responsibilities	Challenges
National Water Supply and Drainage Board	Provide safe drinking water Facilitating the provision of sanitation	Limited funds and large capital associated with sewered system Limited responsibility up to implementation of sewerage and drainage, after which individual municipal councils are in charge
Private institutions	Provide commercial service for the public	Limited in-depth technical know-how, and tend to be profit-oriented
Hotels and restaurants	Attraction for tourism (local and foreign)	Limited in-depth technical know-how, and dependent on private contractors to provide technology to manage waste Lack of space, leading to little designated space for wastewater treatment facilities Lack of capital, especially among small businesses, to dedicate for treatment facility and private waste management
Hospitals	Provide health services for the public	Lack of obvious direct link between polluted lake and public health Large cost associated with conducting studies on public health

Institutions	Role/Responsibilities	Challenges
General public	Law and order Responsible citizen towards environment	Kandy Lake is too large for individuals to undertake Economic pressures, combined with shortcomings in sanitation infrastructure leading to a fair degree of 'selfish behaviour', e.g., littering, illegal dumping

Fig 3.3 Signboards around Kandy Lake; appeals to keep the lake and city clean.

The Solid Waste Management unit of KMC is responsible for the collection and disposal of solid wastes (Fig. 3.3). The provisions related to solid wastes management in the municipal council ordinance mandates that all street refuse, house refuse, night soil and other similar matter collected shall be the property of the council and the council shall have full power to sell or dispose all such matter. The ordinance also prescribes that the municipal council shall, from time to time, provide places convenient for the proper disposal of all street refuse, house refuse, night-soil or other similar matter.

The building department of the KMC grants a certificate of conformity after construction work is completed. This certifies that the work has been completed as per the approved plans and permit. This certificate is required for obtaining water supply from the National Water Supply and Drainage Board (NWSDB), and electricity supply from the Ceylon Electricity Board. Water and electricity may be provided if necessary during construction, but at higher rates. The rates are reduced after the certificate of conformity is produced. Illegal buildings or premises are not supposed to get water and electricity from the respective institutions.

3.1.3 *Urban Development Authority*

The Urban Development Authority (UDA), a body for planning in major cities in Sri Lanka, deals with the major development plan of Kandy city. The Urban Development Authority Act (No. 4 of 1982) states that 'any development activity should obtain a development permit from the relevant local authorities'. The Buildings Department has the task of approving plans for building houses and looking into giving approval according to the specific reservation limits on building houses near waterways. The act also specifies that waste generated within any premises shall be collected and disposed of in a manner which the authority considers appropriate, so as to safeguard the health of the inhabitants.

The UDA act, in Schedule IV (Form E-Regulation 18) provides for the management of waterways. The UDA act details sewerage norms to be followed to obtain a development permit. It states,

> All sewerage and wastewater outlets shall be connected to an existing sewerage system and the authority may in any particular case require the sewerage and wastewater to be pre-treated to bring them to acceptable standards before being connected to a public sewerage system.

In case of Kandy Lake, where a public sewerage system does not exist, sewerage must be disposed through a septic tank and wastewater should be suitably disposed through a soakage pit.

3.1.4 *Central Environmental Authority*

The CEA issues the Environmental Protection Licence (EPL) to medium and large industries, monitors the effluent discharged, and takes necessary legal action where there is none conformance to safeguard the environment. The CEA has set standards for wastewater discharge. Both the CEA and the Public Health Department (PHD) monitor wastewater discharges. The CEA and the Health Department of the KMC are responsible for monitoring wastewater discharge into the Kandy Lake. The National Environment Act (No. 47 of 1980) prescribes that 'No person shall discharge, deposit or emit waste into the environment or carry on any prescribed activity determined by an order made of the act in circumstances which cause or are likely to cause pollution or noise pollution, otherwise than licence issued by CEA and in accordance with the standards and criteria specified'.

CEA issues annual environmental protection licences. It has been noted, there have been occasions even when hotels have small sewage treatment plants (STPs), they still discharge wastes into the lake to reduce electricity and other running costs. When a treatment system is small, unit cost is high so the small hotels are sometimes unable to bear these costs. The challenges faced by CEA is in terms of monitoring unregulated waste discharges into the lake (often at night), from nearby hotels and other establishments including illegal settlements around the lake.

3.1.5   National Water Supply and Drainage Board

The NWSDB is responsible for the supply of safe drinking water and proper drainage facilities. A law of the Water Supply and Drainage Board (No. 2 of 1974) provides for pumping water from the intake at Mahaweli River, operating and maintaining a water treatment facility, distributing water and collecting payments from customers. The board must also ensure proper drainage in order to protect the water resources. The board does not allow water supply to houses and other premises built illegally, without prior approval or a certificate of conformity.

3.1.6   Public Health Department

According to a public health ordinance, the health department is responsible for the cleanliness of all roads, drains, markets and the environment in general. Implementing the public health policy, monitoring effluent discharge from small scale operations, creating public awareness regarding health issues and taking legal action if necessary when it comes to public health and sanitation, are all responsibilities of the health department. The Public Health Inspectors (PHI) are ground level implementing officers of the health department. Legal actions for non-compliance can be taken by the PHI, but actions against polluters, particularly government establishments like the prison and hospital, are a challenge for the PHI.

3.1.7   *Irrigation Department*

The Irrigation Department is responsible for water bodies other than the Mahaweli River. Kandy Lake comes under the Irrigation Department according to an Irrigation Ordinance (No. 32 of 1946). Maintaining the lake boundaries and monitoring the influent and effluent are some of the responsibilities of the department.

3.1.8   *University of Peradeniya and Institute of Fundamental Studies*

University of Peradeniya located 8 km away from Kandy Lake has the mandate to be excellent in knowledge and human resource development at graduate and postgraduate programme levels. Many researchers and students from University of Peradeniya have been conducting studies related to Kandy Lake. Another premier institute that has undertaken research related to Kandy Lake and published articles on Kandy Lake pollution is the National Institute of Fundamental Studies, that was initially based in Colombo when it was established in 1981 and relocated to Kandy in 1985.

3.1.9   *Other Stakeholders*

Apart from these stakeholders, the island at the centre of the lake is managed by the Archaeology Department. A recreational boat house is maintained around the lake by KMC. The flora around the lake is maintained by the Forestry Department and the Royal Botanical Gardens, Peradeniya. The fish species in the lake are monitored by The National Aquatic Resources Research and Development Agency (NARA)—the key national agency responsible for conducting research, development and management of activities related to aquatic resources in Sri Lanka. A master plan for Kandy Lake was developed by the Irrigation Department in 2015 and involved activities such as decorative wall, rehabilitation of pavements, embankment construction, desilting silt traps, dredging, gabion walls to protect the banks, footwalls, pollution traps, wetlands at the estuaries and temperature differential induced siphoning of deep waters. A lakeside walkability project has been started recently by the Ministry of Megapolis and Western Development.

3.2   Institutional Synergies and Conflicts for Lake Pollution Management

Nobody purposely wants to spoil the Kandy Lake. Primarily it is an externality of economic priorities. Although there is civic responsibility not to pollute the Lake, however perhaps there is a fair degree of selfishness among individuals that results in the Lake's pollution.

Late Prof. S.K. Hennayake, UOP

Kandy (institutions, businesses) have wastewater treatment plants, but operation of these is often off. Sometimes there is not enough commitment to maintain or even to design properly. People have also not been so aware on how to manage institutional wastewater.

Dr S.K. Weragoda, NWSDB

Construction in the tropics is tough. Technology selection, workers management, competitive price . . . Hotels and restaurants, usually they do not want to have it (wastewater treatment plants), but because the regulations are strict, they have no choice. They don't like to spend money on treatment plants. And then there is the space problem. In the design process (of a building), sometimes there is no space for a full out wastewater treatment plan, especially when retrofitting houses into hotels. Then, it will be a problem. They may not put staff to maintain the treatment plant. Only when it is time for renewal, then they call for experts or contractors.

Mr. Suranga Manohara, Chairman, Agelta Pvt Ltd

Cost must be affordable, maintenance must be something a layperson can understand and user-friendly. They (clients) want as little maintenance as possible, they have other things to look after . . . In many cases of plant failure, it is because maintenance and service has not been done by the service provider.

Mr. Dananjaya Kuruppu, Managing Director, Enviromec Pvt Ltd

Small-medium enterprises sometimes work on narrow profit margins, not so strong financially. So, they are very concerned with electricity cost, facility cost . . .

Dr R.S.M.K. Rathnayake, Director (Pollution Control), CEA

As a non-profit institution, how to manage, we have so many things to do . . . We don't have funds for a treatment plant, but we cannot dispose to the lake as well, so we have to call the gully bowsers.

Mr. C.W. Karunarathne, Chief Secretary, Sri Dalada Maligawa

While the perceived importance of Kandy Lake has only grown in people's minds, be it the civil society or the government, its management is far from being simplistic owing to the complex stakeholder dynamics influencing a lake nested within a developing city.

All Crown land (state land) and site of the lower lake (Bogambara) were handed to KMC but the lake was not similarly transferred since the old MC Ordinance 16 of 1865 (Section 61) did not authorise it. The lake comes under the Government Agent of Kandy, now called the District Secretary. The roads around the lake are managed by the Department of Highways, the feeder streams maintained by the Irrigation Department, and the sidewalk and pavements around the lake are maintained by the KMC. As there were problems in co-ordinating activities at Kandy Lake, a committee was appointed in the late nineties (headed by the Governor) to look after its development and protection.

During this period, algae blooms appeared in Kandy Lake and the Co-ordinating Committee took remedial action to solve this problem. As there were a number of hotels and guesthouses around the lake it was determined sewage discharge had contributed to the algal blooms.[1] The committee had focused on four areas—the lake water, structures, lake bed and catchment area. The immediate action for the committee was to remove the algal growth and find a long-term solution to mitigate the pollution.[2] The Committee held regular meetings for monitoring of the lake with updates on the number of fishes, growth rates and algal growth among other related issues.

Kandy Lake was under the management of the KMC until 1996. Management of Kandy Lake was then taken over by the Department of Irrigation from 1996. Even though the lake is not a source of irrigation water, the experience of lake maintenance embodied in the Irrigation Department was a

---

[1] Retrieved from http://www.unescobkk.org/fileadmin/user_upload/culture/Tourism/kandy-3.pdf

[2] Looking like a lake once again. http://www.sundaytimes.lk/061105/KandyTimes/kt25.html

Fig 3.4 Desilting at Kandy Lake.

contributory reason for the transfer. As part of its maintenance activities, the Department of Irrigation performs upkeep of the embankment, pavement and 'Cloud Wall', clearing of debris in the Lake, and desilting of the minor and major silt traps (Fig. 3.4).

The Irrigation Department has often been blamed for not adequately controlling pollution in Kandy Lake but this has not taken into account of the many authorities responsible upstream. The challenges are multi-faceted and urban development priorities can take precedence. There is no single coordinated pollution monitoring system at the lake. While CEA has been conducting periodic monitoring of water quality in the lake, the Irrigation Department has recently started its own laboratory for lake water quality monitoring. The universities also periodically collect water samples for various studies.

Dumping of wastes by nearby establishments is common during the rainy season, followed by consequent high pollutant concentration in the dry season. Furthermore, Kandy Lake is a relatively stagnant waterbody and in the dry season pollutant concentrations become high because of the low dilution factor and this had led to algal blooms. The commonly used method of periodical dredging or other mechanical methods to aerate the lake have proved costly owing to the lake morphology and the large amount of bottom sediments.

Line institutions including the Municipal Council, the UDA and the Central Cultural Fund have worked together since World Heritage status was granted to better build urban conservation and the necessary management policies and instruments. Promoting architectural, landscape and environmental quality, as well as developing urban facilities in conservation areas were among the key objectives in the Kandy development plan. The implementation of zoning, development control and building guidelines have contributed to protecting the integrity of the historic areas (UNESCO, 2016). The heritage status however also makes it difficult to implement physical alterations to the city landscape (via digging or constructions), thereby also limiting the options of any major structural interventions for pollution remediation efforts in and around the lake.

The fragmented efforts to manage lake pollution over the years did not garner enough sustained attention from the public and consequently did not encourage their close association with lake pollution management initiatives. In the past, while the lake was once used as a secondary reservoir for the Kandy municipality water system, it was common to find passers-by throwing waste matter into the lake, perhaps ignorant of the damage to the lake ecology and the water quality (Jinadasa et al., 2012). Following the algal bloom episodes, several groups have studied the causes. These have been accompanied with different theories on the fish deaths (discussed in Chapter 4). This lack of definition of the cause had unfortunately made it difficult to choose or commit to an appropriate strategy to prevent future fish mortality.

CHAPTER 4

URBAN LAKES IN CHANGING SOCIO-ECONOMIC AND ENVIRONMENTAL CONTEXTS

The value of the Lake has changed over time. Since it is no longer a drinking water source it primarily holds aesthetic value today.

Prof. Mallika Pinnawala, Department of Sociology, UOP

4.1   The Ever-Changing Kandy City

Despite Kandy city's cultural life and tourism-driven economy, inadequately regulated urbanisation including inadequate waste man-agement facilities have resulted in pollution of the lake—a key tourist attraction. Figure 4.1 presents a timeline of critical events in Sri Lanka and Kandy's history and development that have shaped Kandy city and Kandy Lake, and in many ways also influenced the factors contributing to the issue of pollution.

The advent of the fourth century saw the Tooth Relic brought to Sri Lanka. As the southern tip of Sri Lanka's 'Cultural Triangle', the city of Kandy has been the cultural capital of the country since its founding in the

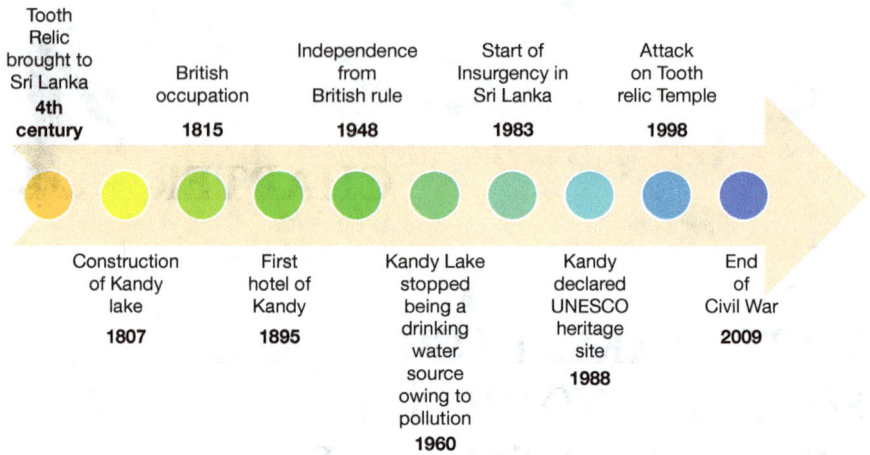

Fig 4.1 Timeline of critical events in Kandy's history and development.

14th century and the last seat of the royal power until British occupation in 1815. Kandy was identified as a UNESCO World Heritage site in 1988.[1]

In the 1940s . . . there were turtles around the Kandy Lake. These gradually disappeared as the city urbanised

Mr. M.G. Gunarathne, Kandy resident (82 years old)

Many changes to the Kandy city landscape occurred during British rule. Hotels started emerging towards the end of the 18th century. Rising pollution levels ceased water withdrawal from Kandy Lake around the 1960s. The year 1983 saw the rise of civil unrest in the country. With the end of the civil war in 2009, hotels grew and many houses converted to guesthouses to take advantage of the inflow of local and international tourists. Today, nearly 4,000 buses pass through Kandy city on a daily basis, of which only 2,000 terminate in the city.

The majority of natural streams that flow through cities in developing countries that are densely populated and urbanised have been converted into wastewater canals. Natural streams suffer pollution from dumping of solid wastes and discharge of wastewaters from multiple sources.

---

[1] https://whc.unesco.org/en/list/450.

The discharge of untreated or inadequately treated wastewaters into waterbodies such as lakes and rivers can have, in many instances, exceeded the pollutant load-carrying capacities of these waterbodies (Mowjood and Sasikala, 2011).

The sanitation infrastructure in rapidly growing Asian cities like Kandy struggle with aging and outdated infrastructure and are often unable to keep pace with the population growth pressure and subsequent waste management needs. Space planning for sanitation may be compromised or shelved because economic development takes priority. The need for large capital investments to implement such infrastructure projects can often be an issue in developing nations. Even when the preceding are not issues, locating the sanitation infrastructure (e.g., a landfill, incineration plant, sewerage lines, sewage treatment plants [STPs]) can lead to acrimonious arguments amongst the various stakeholders. The Kandy City Wastewater Management Project was conceived in 1997 with support from the Finland Government. The project was never realised at the time owing to issues pertaining to siting of the wastewater treatment plant. There was resistance from communities and religious entities who were concerned with odours emanating from the plant, conflicting claims on land ownership to construct pumping stations and proximity of some proposed sites with riparian zone (NWSDB, 2016).

In this respect waterways often become and remain easy and inexpensive places to dump wastewater, and such ease follows from geography where their low elevation facilitates drainage into them (Mowjood and Sasikala, 2011). Large influx of waste inevitably exceeds the natural capacity of the lake to clean itself. The latter is affected by how the lake is recharged and discharges. The Kandy Lake is only recharged through runoff and drainage from its surrounding catchment and the outflow is controlled by sluice gates leading to the Mid-Canal.

In developing countries like Sri Lanka, water resources are also subjected to conflicting water demands for domestic and industrial uses, health and sanitation, inland fisheries, hydropower generation and recreational activities. Such countries often struggle with provision of proper sewage collection and treatment systems due to financial constraints, and it is not uncommon that large volumes of untreated wastewater are directly dumped into nearby waterbodies, including lakes (Jinadasa et al., 2012).

In the 1970s, Sri Lanka opened the economy. One of the benefits of the economic development is Kandy became a tourist place, but the downside is environmental damage.

Late Prof. S.K. Hennayake, UOP

Increased economic opportunities and the pleasant weather attracted many people to Kandy city over the decades. Kandy has one of the best health care facilities in Sri Lanka as it houses many medical specialists. The city is thus visited by numerous patients and their relatives on a daily basis. The emergence of Peradeniya from a suburban town to a 'University village' can be attributed to medical specialists drawn from different parts of Sri Lanka and the training of new ones. With the movement of people, the city had also witnessed the rise of major national and international banks (KMC, 2000).

Modernisation of Kandy in recent years has resulted in many development activities around the lake such as the Kandy city centre and hotels. However, action has been taken by the authorities to slow these to reduce the adverse impact of modernisation on Kandy. Several measures have been adopted to protect sites of historical value. This includes banning the demolition of heritage buildings that are very close to the road but this had prevented road expansion (necessary to alleviate traffic congestion) and other essential development activities.

Kandy Lake is recharged through rainwater, runoff and drainage from Kandy city, and discharges through a sluice gate into the Mid-Canal. The flushing rate is therefore low, and the lake is a relatively stagnant waterbody with minimal dilution of pollution, especially in the dry season. Some pollutants entering the lake may also persist as they settle to the lake bottom, or get adsorbed onto the surface of solids in the sediments. Kandy Lake has a depression point in the lake bed where a large quantity of such sediments has accumulated over time. As the organic matters in the sediment degrade, nutrients are released into the water column.

At the early phase of the project where studies of the Kandy Lake-Mid-Canal systems were conducted and hydraulic modelling of the lake was done (Figs 4.2 and 4.3), it was determined that the lake profile and its hydraulics would result in dead zones where nutrients and pollutants accumulated, with little chance of being flushed out of the system.

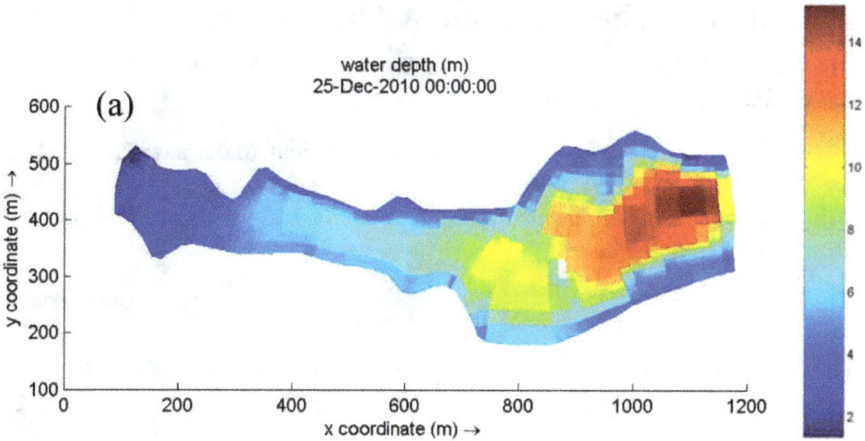

Fig 4.2 Computer simulation of the Kandy Lake showing its depth profile (Pu et al., 2011).

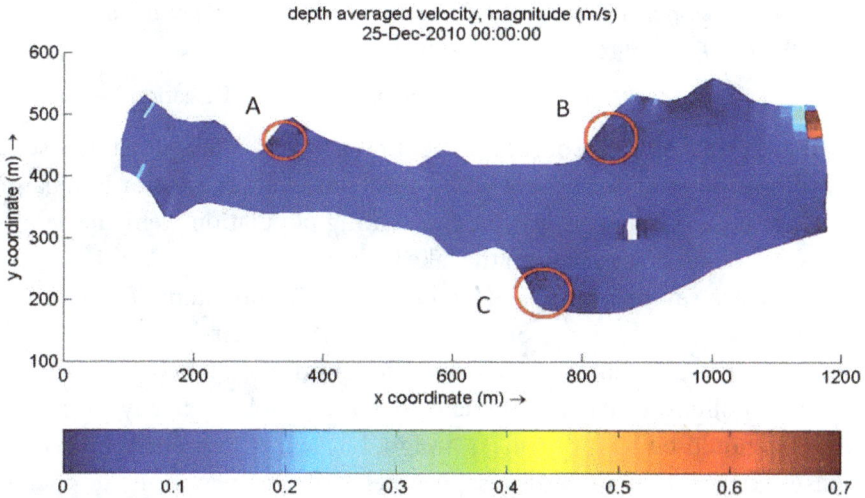

Fig 4.3 Computer simulation of the Kandy Lake indicating location of the dead zones (Pu et al., 2011).

4.2   Kandy Lake Pollution: A Multi-Faceted Problem

After the algal blooms in 2000, the bad smell was obvious. The Mahamaya Girls College had to be closed for two weeks.

Mrs. I. Witthanachchi, Principal, Mahamaya Girls College

Even passers-by sitting in the public buses crossing the Lake could smell the foul odour coming from the Lake.

Kandy resident

After the 1980s, pollution from upstream was very bad; there were 190 hotels.

Dr. S.K. Weragoda, NWSDB

. . . Settlements will empty their septic tanks into the Mid-Canal for the rain to flush away.

Mr. L.L.A. Peiris, Strategic City Development Project Deputy Project Director, Ministry of Megapolis & Western Development

During rainy season, everything comes to Kandy Lake. Garbage accumulated during the dry season are thrown to be washed off by the rain.

Ms. Chandani Devendra, Irrigation Department

As the city expanded, sources of pollution into the lake included solid wastes and wastewater generated by residents, the Sri Dalada Maligawa, hotels and their tourist residents, the floating population, vehicular emissions and boating activities on the lake (Fig. 4.4).

There are several sources of pollution for the pollutants entering the Kandy Lake. In addition, some changes in Kandy city's landscape have occurred in ways that have not been followed simultaneously with the required pollution management efforts. For example, typically for hotels, an STP should be included in its design, but sometimes when individual houses convert into a guesthouse or hotel, these may continue to operate without an STP onsite due to lack of space to construct one (not included in the original layout), but often also due to the costs associated with the STP construction and operation. Hotels often collect their wastes in septic tanks and during rains these are released into the lake, transferring high amounts of nitrogen and phosphorus in the process.

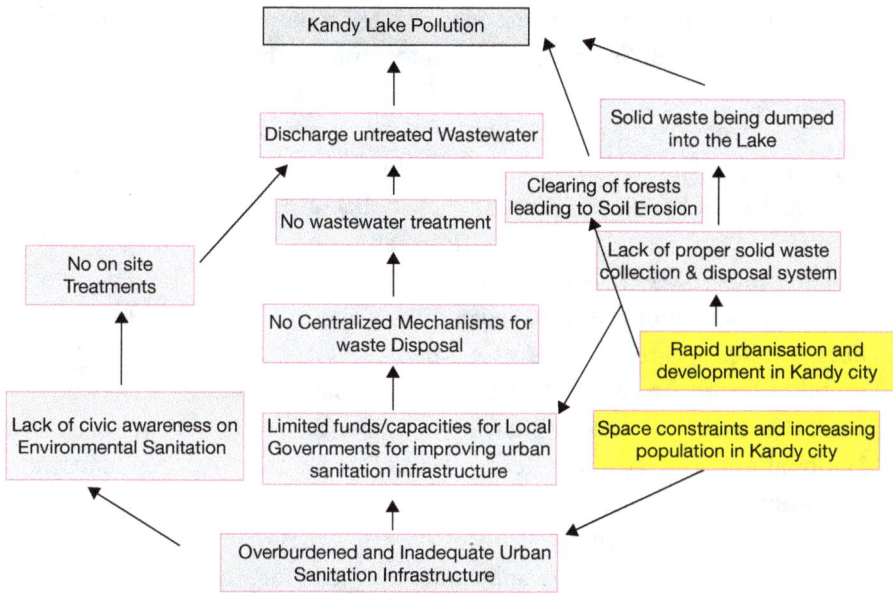

Fig 4.4 Causes of the water quality deterioration in Kandy Lake.

A key source of pollution into the lake was the Temple of the Tooth itself. Hundreds of pilgrims and staff members of the Maligawa use sanitary and other facilities therein daily. Usually, many food and other items are offered to the Dalada Maligawa daily by devotees throughout the year. During festival season, the city becomes severely crowded with pilgrims, sightseers, tourists and others, and the lake becomes a casual dumping ground for garbage. Temporary latrines would then be constructed to cater to the influx of visitors during these period but these are positioned very close to the lake (Jinadasa et al., 2011).

Several studies have been conducted to investigate water quality in the lake (Dissanayake et al., 1982; Silva, 2003; Jayatissa et al., 2006; Guruge et al., 2007). The water quality in the Mid-Canal was monitored by Dissanayake et al. (1987) and canal water and nearby drinking water wells samples were analysed. The drinking wells near the canal showed high concentrations of metals, in some cases exceeding the maximum limits recommended by the World Health Organization. Toxic cyanobacteria had also been detected in Kandy Lake (Jayatissa et al., 2006). This indicate the potential for high-risk situations arising from toxigenic cyanobacterial blooms. Another study had found nine perfluoro surfactants in concentrations between low picograms to low nanograms per litre in Kandy Lake (Guruge et al., 2007).

The lack of mixing generates bottom anoxia which is lethal to all aerobic organisms, and has led to fish deaths in the past.[2] The major algal blooms of 1999 in Kandy Lake were caused by cyanobacteria *Microcystis aeruginosa,* an incident that quickly gained national attention. Silva (2003) had argued that the most likely reason for the sudden emergence of the algal bloom was the lowering of the water level during the dry spell of 1999 that may have resulted in greater access for *Microcystis aeruginosa* to phosphorous mobilised from the anoxic deeper layer (*Microcystis* is known to be buoyant and drifts with the wind on the water surface). According to a report by the National Aquatic Resources Research and Development Agency, fish deaths in Kandy Lake occurred due to the overpopulation of fish, resulting in low oxygen levels and multiplication of parasites arriving with the wastewater discharged into the lake. Subsequently, plans for wastewater treatment plants to purify wastewater were considered to be the most appropriate and technically feasible option. These plans were, however, halted owing to space and the budget constraints required for implementation.

---

[2] http://sundaytimes.lk/091108/ News/nws_24.html.

CHAPTER 5

DESIGN AND IMPLEMENTATION OF SOLUTIONS FOR KANDY LAKE POLLUTION MANAGEMENT

The complex environmental challenges of today . . . will not be solved only by technological expertise. Culture and religion are important determinants of human behaviour, behavioural change and moral responsibility.

UNEP (2016)

A lot of solutions were trialled . . . all projects were done in good faith. However, no integrated action at that time, and after a while, the (Kandy Lake) problem is forgotten. Because of this project, we could connect the people.

Mr L.L.A Peiris, Deputy Project Director, Strategic Cities Development Project, Ministry of Megapolis & Western Development

When (sanitation) systems are needed, it is not there. For example, when people have to go to the toilet; we cannot stop them. The system, then must be able to take the sewage away from the Lake. Your project is giving people that system.

Late Prof. S.K Hennayake, UOP, talking about the UOP-NTU project

This chapter explains the implementation of solutions that were designed to address pollution in Kandy Lake and Mid-Canal, within the framework of a non-profit bilateral collaboration of the two academic institutions—the University of Peradeniya (UOP), Sri Lanka and Nanyang Technological

University (NTU), Singapore. The project was started in 2010 and completed in 2014. This chapter details the process of development of technology-based solutions while adapting these to local cultural and aesthetic needs and preferences, and eventually the process of handing the completed project over to the Kandy stakeholders.

5.1 Challenges for Lake Pollution Management

As with many other tropical lakes, Kandy Lake pollution management efforts have been constrained by inherent challenges and external—largely anthropological—dynamics. Inherent challenges include the tropical setting itself, the lake's physical morphology (discussed in Chapter 2), the lake being a shared resource, and the lake's incapacity to speak for itself, save for the periodical 'silent protests' manifested in events such as algal blooms and mass fish deaths. External factors include rapid urbanisation, landscape transformations, changing socio-cultural values, historical events (discussed in Chapter 2) as well as institutional set-ups (discussed in Chapter 3) for its management. Political instability, too affected lake management as with many other things in a country, although this is beyond the scope of this book.

The anthropological dynamics in an urban lake catchment arguably affects the lake's condition as much or even more than the lake's natural sensitivity. Urban lake pollution is often reflective of the race between development of urban sanitation and economic development. More often than not, especially in old and heritage cities, the former lags behind.

Urban waterways do eventually receive attention, especially when situations have deteriorated severely, for example, the Great Stink in London 1858, and for Kandy Lake, the odour issue in 2001 and mass fish death in 2009. Pollution mitigation actions were then taken, but due to various constraints, solutions were often temporary (e.g., periodic de-silting of Kandy Lake), cosmetic, or those that simply acted to move problems from one place to another (e.g., in 1873, laundry activities in Kandy Lake were prohibited, and instead moved downstream of the Lake spillway, i.e., by the Mid-Canal—perhaps as the Mid-Canal pollution was seen as of less priority then).

Second, as situations change, often new problems emerge (e.g., synthetic chemicals and heavy metals associated with industrial and urban wastes) and age-old problems resurface in greater scale (e.g., amount of silt enter-ing lakes increase as more forests are cleared for development). As such, solutions too must keep pace.

The problem of pollution had nonetheless remained inadequately addressed as it requires concerted and sustained action by the collective of various stakeholders, and owing to the multiplicity of factors that has led to the pollution itself, as well as their dynamic nature over time.

Some of these challenges to effective pollution management efforts in Kandy Lake included:

1. Diffused sources of pollution, economic pressure among residents and lack of off-site treatment options. The costs associated with sewage treatment plant (STP) construction and operation is considered pro-hibitive by owners of small businesses with small profit margins. In absence of viable options, business establishments and perhaps house-holds resort to the illegal practice of emptying their wastes in septic tanks (and gully suckers) into the lake.
2. Space constraints: Kandy city is surrounded by hills, and virtually cannot expand outward. A sewerage project initiated in the 1980s stalled because a site to construct the centralised wastewater treat-ment plant could not be secured. Space was costly and scarce, and residents were reluctant to have a wastewater treatment plant close to their houses.
3. Perceived unavailability of appropriate technology: There was widespread perception that wastewater treatment plants have large area requirements. The many treatment plant failures have also not engendered confidence notwithstanding the reasons for such failure—such as inadequate design and maintenance. Consequently, enforce-ment of Environmental Protection Licence requiring installation and operation of treatment plants would have been difficult.
4. Heritage site preservation: Owing to the UNESCO heritage city status given to Kandy, there were restrictions to altering the landscape around and in the lake.
5. Lake morphology: The Kandy Lake, is a relatively stagnant waterbody with a deep part where mixing of the water column is limited. The com-monly used method of periodical dredging or mechanical aeration of the lake had proved costly.

6. Lack of concerted and sustained efforts: Fragmented efforts have not garnered enough sustained attention from the public and so did not receive their close involvement and support. The algal bloom episodes did attract attention, but the absence of consensus over cause and solution had not helped in the problem's resolution. Urban lake pollution may seem deceivingly simple at the surface if ground conditions are not adequately considered. Placing excessive emphasis on the technical know-how and technology would not suffice. Local culture, social behaviour, values, attitudes, norms, economics, politics and layers of history often set the stage. It is important, then for one to be aware of the complex issues faced by the community and empathise with them, when designing solutions. Projects attempting to address urban lake pollution management, therefore have to be set within a framework cognizant of the local challenges.

In cognizance of the challenges to Kandy Lake pollution remediation (discussed in Chapters 3 and 4), the group of researchers at UOP and NTU realised that the solution to be designed for Kandy Lake pollution management had to be set within a framework which can be effective and sustainable over time. This framework included the following features:

- It had to engage and have the approval and consensus of multiple relevant stakeholders.
- Technology implementation, operations and upkeep must be supportable locally, that is, could be carried out by local contractors using locally available parts and materials. The technology must work to restore confidence of the public that wastewater treatment for Kandy city is not impossible.
- Solutions had to be acceptable by the community and manageable by local governmental authorities for continued operation. To this end, a sense of ownership needed to be cultivated and as such, local stakeholders must be involved in solution development and decision-making. Solutions must also take into account cultural preferences and sensitivities.
- It had to consider local capacities to sustain the project on their human and fiscal resources over the long term, as lake pollution remediation often needs sustained efforts, spanning years wherein there can be

changes in the authorities, funding, policy etc. In other words, it had to be mindful of the local economics.

- It had to consider and implement actions to prepare the local stakeholders (i.e., in terms of administrative and technical capacity) for the responsibility required of them to sustain the solution following departure of the original project team.
- It had to consider the space constraints in Kandy.
- It had to preserve the cultural space around Kandy Lake and be circumspect of Kandy city's world heritage status. Installations close to the lake and in the lake must at least aesthetically blend with the surroundings.

The project's attempts in addressing the above are discussed in the following section.

5.2   Overall Approach

5.2.1   *Stakeholder Engagement*

There was generalisation that universities tend to not do a good job (in development work), because they have no flexibility to also consider the requestor's requirements, and that they only do academic work which is not practical.

Dr Shameen Jinadasa, Senior Lecturer, UOP

A lot of pollution comes from people outside, not Kandy residents. Sometimes people come to the lake to feed the fish as an act of kindness. While influential, the Sri Dalada Maligawa also couldn't endorse something sounding so counterintuitive (i.e. not to feed the fish in Kandy Lake)

Dr G.B.B Herath, Senior Lecturer, UOP

While universities have in-depth scientific and possibly technical knowledge, where problems require full-scale implementation of technology, they may not be the party of first choice, as clients (public and private alike) typically would seek companies with established track record of practice. In addition, university-led projects tend to stop short of full-scale implementation as (1) official permits to set up permanent facilities outside of the university will be needed, and consequently stakeholder buy-in is required, which takes time and long-term commitment; (2) funding available to the institutions may be limited to research activities; and (3) as universities are increasingly judged by academic research and consequently publications, their attention tends to be directed to exactly that with diminished interest in practical applications.

Hence, when the group of researchers from the UOP and NTU initiated the project 'Mitigation of Pollution at Kandy Lake and Mid-Canal, Sri Lanka', the group was aware that there were several layers of stakeholders that ought to be engaged and had to be convinced: political, institutional, individuals and the ultimate beneficiaries—general public beyond the project's immediate circle.

The local authorities and the government must be made part of the team. This is primarily because the project's installations in Kandy city and Kandy Lake would ultimately need their permission and would benefit from the local authorities' experience of on ground implementation. Second, the project was intended for the benefit of the public, in alignment with the interest and directions of the local authorities. Finally, beyond the project's seed funding, both universities would not have the financial and manpower capacity to sustain the long-term operation and maintenance of the systems installed.

Key personnel of government agencies and Kandy authorities were involved in discussions since the project's inception in 2010. These included the Chief Engineers, Engineers and Directors from the National Water Supply and Drainage Board ('Water Board'/ NWSDB), Irrigation Department (ID), Kandy Region, Kandy Municipal Council (KMC) and the Central Environment Authority (CEA). Many were personally involved in the activities of the project, including but not limited to

- Broad study of the problems, and subsequent scoping of the in-depth study and implementation
- Regular updates to key decision-makers
- Community surveys and field research
- Assessments of designs and technical proposals of local contractors
- On-site supervision during construction
- Approval for in-kind contributions such as access and provision of space for project requirements, and manpower
- Several engineers from the Water Board, ID and KMC were also pursuing part-time postgraduate degrees at the UOP at the time of the project, and their thesis work became coupled with the project

Presence of the various local stakeholders also lent legitimacy to the project, especially during the group's first meeting (Figs. 5.1–5.4) and subsequent updates with the Kandy Governor, from whom approval was required. It must be noted that prior to the project, there was already a Kandy Lake Management Committee set up and led by the Governor. Notwithstanding the support rendered by the various parties, the message that the project is a high-stake undertaking was clearly articulated to the project team—failure would have been highly visible and consequential. A key reason for this was Kandy Lake's proximity to and association with the Sri Dalada Maligawa, a 'National Treasure'.

Beyond political and official consents, there was also a need to obtain the trust and consent of individual institutional stakeholders. This included both the UOP and the NTU themselves, as the project was indeed a risky undertaking, with both institutions' established reputations at stake. In addition, managing such projects in terms of administration was distinct from typical university activities. In the case of the UOP, the Faculty of Engineering which led the project had to obtain special permission from

Fig 5.1 First project meeting at the University of Peradeniya (UOP).

Fig 5.2 Briefing prior to socio-economic survey at Mid-Canal, led by Mrs. S.K.I. Wijewardena, Former Chief Engineer, Kandy Municipal Council.

Fig 5.3 Stakeholders meeting with the Governor.

Fig 5.4 Signing of Memorandum of Understanding between University of Peradeniya (UOP) and Nanyang Technological University (NTU).

the Vice-Chancellor. Similarly, collaborations proposed for approval by the NTU had to demonstrate significant academic value and quality.

Especially important, however were buy-ins from institutions which would be custodians of the project outputs, that is, the Sri Dalada Maligawa and the Mahamaya Girls' College (MGC). For instance, while the Dalada Maligawa agreed to have an STP built for them through the project, one could imagine the anxiety of the temple's management as there was already a plant previously commissioned but which had failed and was then defunct.

With MGC, the primary concern was whether the college would be able to independently sustain the programme introduced by the project and make full use of the facility (an outdoor classroom), as these may be seen as 'extra-curricular' and hence 'distracting'. While events and activities could be initiated during the course of the project, in absence of external funding, there was risk that these could not recur and be sustained.

Despite all the uncertainties, at a certain point in a project, the group had to take the plunge and allow the project to move, as there were time limits, budgets and targets committed to—on top of good faith. To some extent, such risk-taking ultimately relied on all the individuals involved in the project having confidence in each other, and this would mean that in such a project, team member selection is as important as technology selection, if not more critical.

And finally, in order to appeal broadly and to increase awareness of the general public, the project must be significantly visible. At one level, it is literal; installations in and around Kandy Lake must not conflict with the cultural and natural appeal of the place. It indeed helped that Kandy Lake is right at the centre of Kandy city and is surrounded by places of attractions and busy traffic (and yet visibility means that should failure happen, it will be no less noticeable). At another level, the message and learning from the project must be regularly articulated at various forums. The educational institutions, that is, the UOP and the MGC played major roles in educating the future generations, while the local authorities held the responsibility to carry out public outreach and education.

5.2.2   Pollutant Mitigation at Source

Kitchen wastewater used to go directly to the [Kandy Lake]. During Poya (full moon) days, two gully bowsers would be needed. When gully bowsers come in to the temple, it is a very embarrassing situation, unpleasant experience for the people.

Mr. W.M.G.A. Bandara, Secretary, Sri Dalada Maligawa

Sometimes the (Temple) visitors are from universities from England, Australia, India, school children and hotel owners. On the way to the toilet they happen to see the Sewage Treatment Plant. Some of them ask me how the plant was designed and is operated and I explain it to them with great pride.

Mr. Senevirathne, STP operator at Dalada Maligawa & electrician in Sri Lankan army (on special duty for STP operation)

The project team and local authorities in Kandy were aware that it will be impossible to clean Kandy Lake if sewage discharges into it continued. At the time the project started in 2010, the Kandy City Wastewater Management Project, led by the National Water Supply and Drainage Board had just been initiated. However, securing space where a centralised wastewater treatment plant could be built was a challenge, as most residents were resistant to having a STP sited close in their neighbourhoods. Hence, in the meantime, wastewater from Kandy city, treated or otherwise, continued to be drained into Kandy Lake and Mid-Canal.

Although institutions and commercial establishments are required to treat their wastewater prior to discharge, many of the treatment facilities are not in good working condition. Total management of wastewater within the Kandy Lake catchment would have required a scale of manpower and funding resources beyond the capacity of the two universities to accommodate. It was therefore decided to select one technology and commission only one treatment plant, to serve as a model to demonstrate that effective wastewater treatment can be achieved and economically so.

The Sri Dalada Maligawa was then approached to serve as host for the plant. This was in consideration of its proximity to the lake, prominence and influence in the eyes of the public, the large number of visitors it hosts, and the wastewater it generates. The area around the outlet from Maligawa was found to be among the most polluted areas in Kandy Lake. The sewage treatment plant was designed and implemented with support of the Dalada Maligawa, to set an example for other institutions to emulate. Because the existing Dalada Maligawa wastewater treatment plant had failed and could not be rectified, the temple has had to hire gully bowsers to transport away its wastewater. When there are no treatment facilities nearby, wastewater and septic tank sludge removed by the bowsers are disposed at unsanitary dumpsites (and at times, even directly to the Kandy Lake and Mid-Canal), posing public health hazards. Waterborne disease is still one of the top causes of hospitalisation in Sri Lanka.

Before installation of the STP, the kitchen wastes and sewage were discharged to the lake. The volume and strength of wastewater from the Maligawa kitchen was significant. On average, every day 32 kg of rice and 32 types of curries would be prepared for *puja*. Toilet waste was managed by gully bowsers (once per week, and sometimes twice during the festival season). The temple management was aware it could be a major polluter of Kandy Lake. There are two ponds at the entrance to the temple and as these are connected to Kandy Lake, these ponds will also deteriorate as Kandy Lake quality deteriorates.

In spite of the necessity, will and consent of the temple, there was some degree of anxiety with regards to construction of a new wastewater treatment plant:

[The Dalada Maligawa] had expectations from previous plant; they were very scared of giving the [Sewage Treatment Plant] project to some other person. They had issues with smell. Especially during Poya days and alms-giving, a lot of wastewater come in. They had problems selecting a competent technical person.

Mr Dananjaya Kuruppu, Managing Director, Enviromec Pvt Ltd, contractor for the new STP

There were two main kitchens and toilets in the temple, one at the main temple building, and another at the Pilgrim's Rest *'Wishrama Shalawa'*. The project's original plan was to start off with treating only sewage from the main building. This was subsequently revised to include the pilgrim's rest sewage, at the request of the then-Governor and the temple. There was consideration of refurbishing the existing plant and to engage the original contractor, although subsequently, it was decided to have a new plant. In total, three consecutive tender calls for the STP with local engineering, procurement and construction companies were invited. Technical proposals were assessed by a committee assembled by UOP, NTU and the NWSDB. Proposals received in first two calls had to be rejected owing to technical shortcomings.

Finding a site for the STP had required several rounds of site visits and deliberations, due to several factors. First, space was very constrained; it was preferred the plant is located away from the main buildings, just in case of odours. A space close to the police station was later found to be sufficient for a compact plant. Second, excavations are not allowed at most locations within the temple, especially where there are tiled floors (as replacements for the old tiles would have been impossible, and also to avoid possible damage to archaeological assets). Where excavation is allowed, building contractors were not allowed to excavate more than 2 ft from the surface. As a result, it was encouraged to utilise existing pits where possible, and at the same time the shortest and safest routes for pipelines had to be thought of. At several spots, the pipe runs were designed to be laid alongside existing storm water drains. In addition, Kandy is an area with uneven geological formation. Even within a building complex, the land can be undulating (Fig. 5.6). This may pose challenges when building hydraulic structures such as water pipes and wastewater pipes as pumping may then be needed to convey the liquids. Excavations, sometimes need special attention, as the soil in Kandy tend to be loose and prone to slips, and at times within 2 m from surface, big rocks are found.

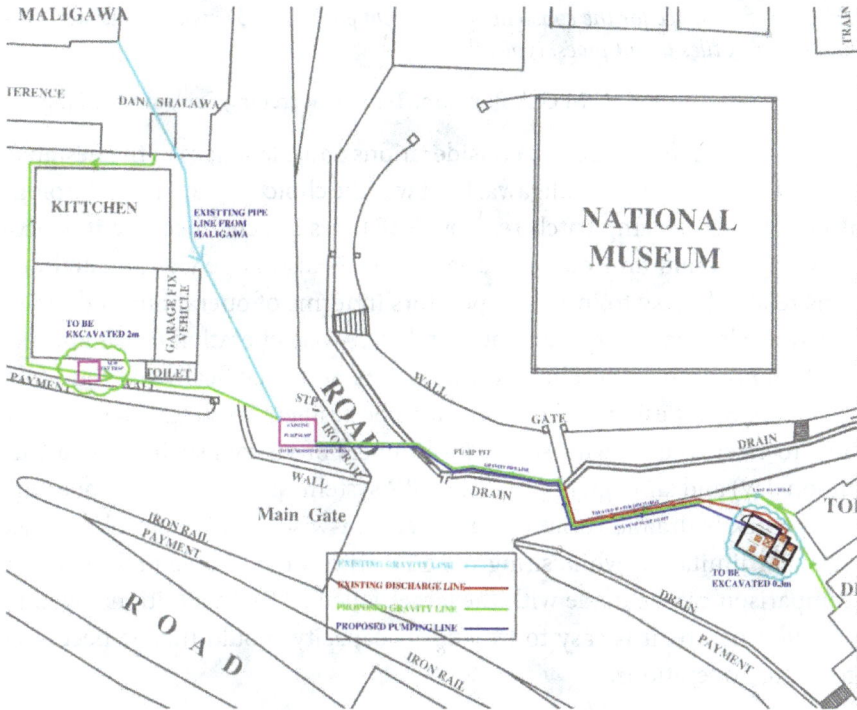

Fig 5.5 Drawing by Enviromec Pvt. Ltd. for Sri Dalada Maligawa, Project: "Sewage Treatment Plant for Sri Dalada Maligawa", 17 September 2013.

Fig 5.6 Excavation of pump sump at existing pit, during a *Poya* day; completed pump sump.

Trying to find space for the construction was not easy... No excavations allowed. We had to break tiles to put pipes, typically.

Mr. W M G A Bandara, Temple Secretary, Sri Dalada Maligawa

There were several design considerations and challenges in the design of the STP for the Dalada Maligawa. First was the choice of the STP technology itself. The sequencing batch reactor (SBR) was selected because it is economical to build and operate. The system is also largely automated and thus relatively easy to instruct operators in terms of operations and maintenance. Electricity requirement with batch-wise operation is less and not continuous . However, above these factors and specifically for the Maligawa, the STP design was developed to be resilient to shock loads and so able to cater to days with spikes in numbers of visitors such as Poya (full moon day) and alms-giving day. The SBR system was designed to cope with such quick hydraulic variations and yet area-wise the SBR took less space (a major limitation while siting the STP within the temple premises, and comparison can be made with the larger failed STP). In addition, given its modular nature, it is easy to expand its capacity should this be necessary for future operations.

Selection of contractors were very tight. Calculations were done, with inputs from different experts.

Dr S.K Weragoda, NWSDB

During construction, regular supervision (Fig. 5.7) was conducted by project team members from the UOP and the Water Board, Dalada Maligawa administration (Chief Secretary and Secretary), in addition to contractor's supervisors. Periodically updates were conveyed to the Governor on the project's progress.

Temple administration had to facilitate access to site, loading and unloading material. Once a week, Dr. Weragoda and I supervised the construction. Sometimes, I drop by the site after sending off my son to school. From time to time, during critical stages we have to check if amount of rebar and concrete strength is correct, and watertightness. Every two weeks, we have a progress meeting with the Temple management.

Dr Shameen Jinadasa, Project PI (UOP)

Fig 5.7 Supervision during construction of the sequencing batch reactor (SBR) by project team and temple secretary.

Fig 5.8 SBR sewage treatment plant during construction and after official inauguration.

Very glad to hear of the completion of the project. Yes I will be there to see the commissioning.

Extract from Governor Tikiri Kobbekaduwa's email reply to Dr Shameen Jinadasa, 7 February 2014

A technician hired by the Dalada Maligawa and trained by the contractor who built the plant oversees day-to-day operation of the plant. The routine included daily removal of grease and scum from the oil and grease (O&G) trap, checking on the pumps and aerators, checking of SBR sludge and the plant effluent colour, and weekly water test. The Dalada Maligawa also assigned periodical maintenance and technical support to the contractor who built the STP.

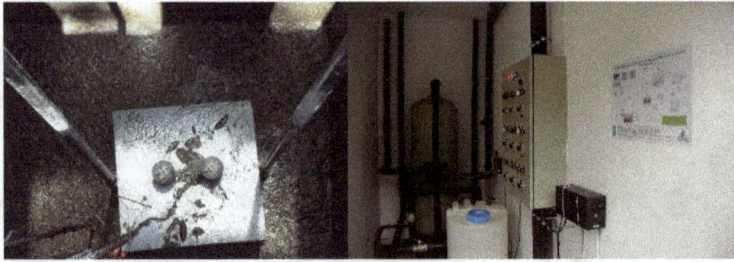

Fig 5.9 (a) Inside the SBR. (b) The control room. (Official project pictures, copyright to authors/NEWRI).

Fig 5.10 Checking electrical equipment at the control room; waste oil accumulates as scum on the O&G trap surface; daily checklist for operator; sample bottles to check colours of the SBR sludge and plant effluent. (Official project pictures, copyright to authors/NEWRI).

Every six hours, water from the oil and grease trap is pumped to the SBR. Every day, I check colour and smell of the sludge and effluent. Water is tested weekly every Wednesday . . . There was no issue the past 1–3 years, except once in 2015 when the washing chemicals were changed. It caused issue to the SBR . . . Aerator was repaired once by the contractor . . .

Mr Senevirathne, STP Technician and Operator, Sri Dalada Maligawa

The STP was commissioned in February 2014, and was officially handed over to Dalada Maligawa administration in July 2014. It was hoped that successful set up of the STP at the Dalada Maligawa would be a model to help to restore trust among the people in Kandy that wastewater treatment situations in Kandy are not impossible and technologies are available and manageable if applied and used properly. Failure of treatment plants often result in unresolved arguments between designer (e.g., inappropriate design), operator (e.g., equipment not maintained) and users (e.g., solid waste flushed down toilets, jamming pipelines, screens or equipment), to the loss of plant owners (having a malfunctioning facility in their backyard). Legal means to resolve these were often not preferred as the capital expense for a facility alone would have cost the owner a large sum, and to pursue compensations legally would cost even more time and money. Hence, at times malfunctioning plants are just shut down and abandoned.

5.2.3   Lake Clean-Up Measures on Site

There was extreme pollution in the past that I see. Now there are flowers floating on the lake, that is something interesting.

Ms. Gayathri Bandaranayake, Mahamaya Girls' College Student

People are very attracted to it (the floating wetlands). I feel personally attached and proud to take care of the project. It makes the lake beautiful . . . The people in my village also commented about it, they are very happy.

Mr. H.A. Sunil Shantakumara, worker, Irrigation Department

It is a very good project, and also very beautiful thing (the wetlands). Even small children ask how we keep the plants floating.

Ms Chandani Devendra, Former Director of Irrigation

It is a combination of construction and nature.

Mr. Suranga Manohara, Chairman, Agelta Pvt Ltd

Considering the hydraulics of Kandy Lake as discussed briefly in Chapter 4, the project team concluded assistive measures for removing existing nutrients from Kandy Lake were required to clean the lake. Several options were considered to address this issue. Prior to the project, Kandy Lake was cleaned through periodical desilting by the Irrigation Department, and to some extent, by water lilies grown in its forebay. With the emergence of additional buildings around the lake there was an increase in the silt entering the lake. The lack of low level sluice gates in Kandy Lake made it difficult to remove the additional silt by flushing. The Irrigation Department previously helped the KMC in dredging operations in 1960s, 1970s and in 1987/1988. Sediments in the Kandy Lake however have significant nutrient and heavy metals content accumulated over many years. If these sediments are not properly disposed they can pollute waterways elsewhere. Similarly, while water lilies help to remove nutrients, they grow fast in nutrient-rich water and typically difficult to control in terms of spread. Further, if the water lilies are not harvested, the nutrients would then be recycled back into the lake.

Mechanical means to assist mixing and aeration of lakes, such as installation of fountains and aerators were also discussed with the local authorities. However, the cost of installation, operations and maintenance of these devices were found to be prohibitive. In addition, there was also requirement to preserve the natural look and feel of the lake, and its heritage value. As such, highly mechanised options were to be avoided where possible.

Considering the above, floating wetlands were designed, tested and installed at the major inlets to Kandy Lake, especially where dead zones are formed, utilising data from the modelling exercise of Kandy Lake as a location guide. The floating wetlands served as a passive lake water treatment and protection system. Floating wetlands were selected because these: (1) take up excess nutrients from the lake and assist trapping of the larger particles without consuming energy; (2) require virtually no land space— which is scarce in Kandy city; (3) are easy to control and maintain, as the plants will not grow outside the float, and the floats can be anchored in place at locations where it can be most effective and this also facilitated harvesting which would remove the nutrients from the lake and avoid recycling and (4) naturally integrate into and beautify the surroundings.

Application of floating wetlands is a relatively new concept in Sri Lanka, although it has been extensively researched at the UOP in collaboration with NTU (Weragoda *et al.*, 2012; Weragoda *et al.*, 2011; Pu *et al.*, 2011). The floating wetlands at Kandy Lake became a pioneering field-scale application in the country. In essence, the wetlands are intended to inter-cept and treat sewage entering the lake. The plants also helped to remove excess nutrients already in the lake, and the roots of the plant aid in trapping suspended solids (much like a filter). The technology was also selected as it blends with the lake's surroundings and furthermore beautifies it when the plants flower. With support from the Irrigation Department (ID) of Sri Lanka, several configurations of floating wetlands were installed at major inlets to the Kandy Lake. Floating Wetlands vary from the other constructed wetland systems since the former employ rooted plants grow-ing on mats floatingon the water surface. The plants do not float freely nor are they rooted in the sediments of the lake.

Constructed wetlands are engineered systems that are designed and constructed to utilise the natural functions of vegetation, soils and their associated microbial assemblages for treating various kinds of wastew-ater (Kadlec and Knight, 1996; Vymazal, 2011). They have convention-ally involved the use of free-floating aquatic plants, or sediment-rooted emergent wetland plants, either with water flowing through the root zone (subsurface flow) or among the stems (surface flow) (Tanner, 1996). How-ever, in many cases, lake restoration using submerged aquatic plants is inevitably restricted by aspects such as water depth, wave motion, water turbidity and transparency, sedimentation etc. (Qin, 2009; Wang *et al.*, 2009).

Floating wetlands was chosen over other technological alternatives for several reasons, technical and non-technical: (1) these were simple to con-struct using locally available material; (2) had less maintenance cost (could be subsumed within the regular budget of the [ID]) compared to other treatment methods; (3) there were no electricity or machinery costs and low costs associated with labour; (4) the only space needed was for prepar-ing the modules of wetlands; (5) the wetlands also provided areas for flora and fauna to flourish including additional breeding grounds for fishes and resting space for waterfowl; (6) there had already been pilot studies and installations at the UOP, and one of the NWSDB engineers had studied it as a postgraduate project. Having seen a technology tested and witnessed its function helped in visualising it in full-scale adoption and hence incul-cated confidence; (7) wetland plant flowers added to the lake's aesthetics, and attracted public attention.

Fig 5.11 Installation of floating wetlands. (Official project pictures, copyright to authors/NEWRI).

Fig 5.12 Installation of floating wetlands. (a) First phase with yellow and red flowers at Mahamaya inlet. (b) Second phase installations with hexagonal float design. (Official project pictures, copyright to authors/NEWRI).

Installations of the floating wetlands started at the largest inlet to Kandy Lake, the Mahamaya inlet, close to MGC. The wetlands were placed along the bridge separator. The first unit trialled was made using bamboo, but it was found to be too heavy and could not carry the weight of as much plants as a float made of polyvinyl chloride (PVC) pipe could. The floats were lined up and anchored to the bridge structure, and subsequently coconut coir was spread onto the mats (as an affordable and common planting media), before planting the young shoots of *Canna iridiflora*.

While *Canna* was not the best wetland plant when it comes to nutrient absorption, it was selected as it is native to Sri Lanka, and it is a flowering

Fig 5.13 Saranankara silt trap upstream to Kandy Lake. One can see oil film on the water, small bits of plastic and accumulated silt. (Official project pictures, copyright to authors/NEWRI).

Fig 5.14 The floating wetlands in Kandy Lake have become a popular photography spot. In the background is the Mahamaya Inlet/Silt Trap. (Official project pictures, copyright to authors/NEWRI).

plant. At the beginning, yellow-orange and red flowers were selected as these colours hold significance to Sri Lanka and Buddhism.

Following the first set of installations, the ID recommended alternative designs for the wetlands, as remaining inlets of Kandy Lake do not have a 'straight-line' structure, unlike the Mahamaya inlet. The ID felt that a more rounded design could be more pleasing considering the natural curvatures of the lake bank. Several shapes were suggested (butterfly-shape, circular) before hexagonal units were chosen considering economics and availability of the 120° PVC Y-joint. There was also the idea of having a wood float in the middle of the module, so that people can stand on the float. However, given the concerns with structural stability and safety, the idea was abandoned. These hexagonal modules have been installed at three inlet locations, including two close to the Dalada Maligawa.

After official completion and handover in July 2014, all floating wetlands are owned and managed by the ID. The *Canna* plants flower after three months, and mature in about six months, after which it would need to be harvested and the mats replanted with new shoots. Upkeep costs of the wetlands are within the IRD's budget for regular maintenance of Kandy Lake. While the floating wetlands cleaned Kandy Lake, there are additional values in the technology. The plants acted as biological indicators indicating progressive lake water clean-up (i.e., healthy plants with beautiful flowers indicated polluted water) of nutrients. Second, its visual appeal drew attention to Kandy Lake which sensitised the residents to any decline in environmental quality. The Mahamaya inlet, for instance is a silt trap. Silt traps in general are not typically attractive: it is an unassuming, functional tank-like structure accumulating muddy deposits from runoffs, protecting water bodies. One might not imagine it can one day be attractive.

5.2.4   *Citizen Engagement, Awareness and Capacity Building*

In Kandy, there is abundance of water. People may have the perception that there is always water . . . There is a stream near my house. Someone passed by and threw a bag of garbage into the stream, not knowing that they will drink this water.

Dr C.S Kalpage, Head of Department (Chemical & Process Engineering), UOP

It was observed that these particular subjects related to water and wastewater . . . were included in the school curriculum, but no emphasis had been given on educating school children to understand their role and responsibilities in these aspects.

Mr. P.H. Sarath Gamini, Wastewater Management & Kandy City Wastewater Management Project

Fig 5.15 Fish feeding beside the lake. (Official project pictures, copyright to authors/NEWRI).

I think it is important for the students that they are really doing something useful. Activities of the Wetland Club give us an opportunity to do something for the environment and society.

Ms. Gayathri, Student & Wetlands Club Member, Mahamaya Girls College

Urban lakes, and their clean-up in general require their users' participation, as the general public often directly (e.g., littering, feeding of water animals) or indirectly (e.g., discharges from households, sewage from production of goods and services) pollute the waterbodies. The perceived value of a waterbody can change over time in the public consciousness. For instance, a clean, pristine lake or river may be highly prized as something to preserve and guard, but waterways which gradually become dumpsites although not originally so, may be seen as a nuisance and serving no purpose. The role of education, across generations, then is important to keep the public aware, informed and engaged in the effort to protect their living environment, of which the urban lake is a part. Long existing habits, such as littering and lake-side fish feeding, had to be discouraged.

We took up the school project for larger societal good and not for monetary value. This project was first of its kind in Sri Lanka and I am proud to be one of the contractors associated with it.

Mr. Suranga, Agelta, responsible for construction of wetland club class at MGC

I consider this project as a service to the temple. There is an emotional effect with this work. Opportunity to contribute, kept a minimum margin of costs.

Mr. Dananjaya Kuruppu, Managing Director, Enviromec Pvt. Ltd (contractor for STP at Dalada Maligawa)

I do my job with my full heart for the Dalada Maligawa and the country.

Mr. Senevirathne, STP operator at Dalada Maligawa & electrician in Sri Lankan army (on special duty for STP operation)

The project had emphasised the local authorities and people are involved in the process of decision-making (and to have the final say) and implementation of the project. Such involvement ensured a greater degree of sense of ownership. From the perspective of costs, it was also not practical, to frequently fly in foreign experts and manpower. Second, because the project will be left in local hands upon completion, it is necessary they are convinced they are the largest stakeholder in the project, its impact and the future of Kandy Lake, Mid-Canal and the Mahaweli River. The UOP's lecturers and students led the activities of the project. Local engineering contractors under the supervision of relevant local authorities (the Water Board and the ID) constructed the facilities. This ensured knowledge of the project design and implementation was transferred and retained by the beneficiaries of the project.

To further enhance public awareness and transfer of knowledge, an extra-curricular program, the 'Wetlands Education Programme' (WEP) was launched at the MGC, a premier school located next to Kandy Lake. This aimed to cultivate environmental stewardship among the students. The WEP idea was fleshed out by a group of undergraduates from NTU and UOP, and is managed by a student club at the MGC (the Wetlands Education Club). The programme is outlined in Table 5.1. Activities within the programme include regular water monitoring and inter-school events. The first of the latter was held in May 2015, titled 'Water, Wetlands, and We' and had participation from ten schools in Kandy. However, it was noted

Table 5.1 Overview of the Wetland Education Programme at Mahamaya Girls' College.

	Scientific Skill Training	Knowledge Module	Awareness Module
Aim	To arm students with hands-on skills, such as observation, monitoring water quality and analysing data	To broaden knowledge of students about wetlands and wastewater management techniques	To help increase awareness to the community especially in reducing water pollution by training the students to be environmental envoys
Description of Activities	• Monitoring of water quality parameters at selected sites	• Site visits • Reading and Sharing of information • Science competitions/fairs	• Activities that engage other schools and the community
Example of Suggested Activities	• Monitoring of water quality at inlets to Kandy Lake • Monitoring of water quality at Mid-Canal • Comparing water qualities of tap water, Kandy Lake, Mid-Canal and school pond	• Lectures/Seminars • Workshops with University of Peradeniya • Poster exhibition • Poster/handout design competition • Mascot/cartoon/logo design competition	• Cleaning up Mid-Canal together with the community • Presentation to other Schools • Wetland information notice board (in school to be maintained by the students) • Maintaining information boards around Kandy Lake regarding the information

(Continued)

Table 5.1 Overview of the Wetland Education Programme at Mahamaya Girls' College. (*Continued*)

	Scientific Skill Training	Knowledge Module	Awareness Module
		• Sharing sessions with the college • Field trips e.g., Visit to Pussellawa or water treatment facilities	Students to become nature guides at Kandy Lake
Remarks	Due to the limited number of advanced monitoring equipment and their cost, students might be limited to the simple monitoring kits	The students should be exposed to all possible type of treatment methods to broaden their minds. It is important to emphasise that wetland may not be the ultimate solution, and source control of pollution is highly desirable	As other schools and the community would be involved in the activities, the school must collaborate with the municipal government and involved authorities. Safety procedures should be observed especially when students act as nature guides or are conducting clean-up of the Mid-Canal. With the sheer number of people, this might be challenging

that to continue the programme, collaboration with and support from the universities and local authorities are needed to augment the limited resources that schools have to support such activities.

An outdoor classroom with models of constructed wetlands was constructed within the school's premises. This outdoor classroom allowed for facilities that would support hands-on learning related to water and the environment. The pond therein provided a focal point where students have the opportunity to get in touch with nature (before reaching out to the lake). The classroom comprised a sheltered lecture room, a pond, shelves to place experiment setups and posters. While initially left open, it had to be protected with chain link fencing subsequently to keep out monkeys which have found their way in.

In total, 21 undergraduates and postgraduates from both universities became involved in the project with some 10 staff from the participating government agencies. The students conducted community surveys, and water testing and determination of wetlands performance, and designed the

Fig 5.16 Glimpses of the outdoor classroom at Mahamaya Girls' college (MGC). (Official project pictures, copyright to authors/NEWRI).

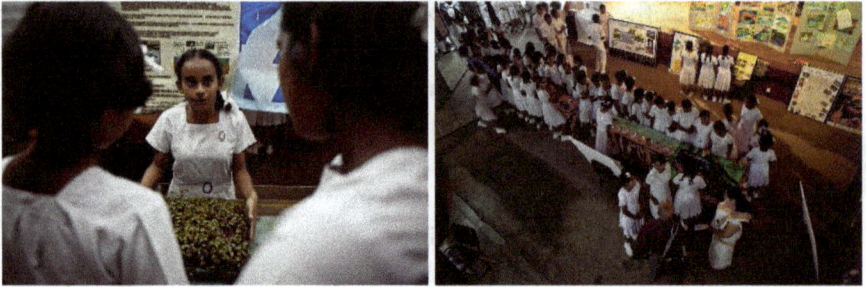

Fig 5.17 School exhibition (Water, Wetland and We) held at the MGC. (Official project pictures, copyright to authors/NEWRI).

school programme at the MGC. (Figs. 5.16 and 5.17) The students benefited from the 'real life' exposure in their work. The students learned to interact with people outside the academic setting. The project also imparted values such as awareness of the environment, pollution and its impact, civic-mindedness and the need for thinking beyond immediate needs. The younger school children learned very quickly and brought what they learned home to their families. It was hoped that this softer approach to exerting influence would have longer lasting effect compared 'coercive' approaches such as prohibiting littering, imposing fines or keeping areas out of bounds.

We had an advantage when we applied for jobs after we graduate, as we have seen real plants, not only in textbooks, and we have had experience interacting and working with the community.

Ms. Wageesha Premarathne, UOP graduate

The other role of education in environmental protection is through formal transfer of knowledge and practical training (in schools and institutes of higher learning) to build capabilities and capacities in the human resources. The latter would be required to support the solutions implemented, and to innovate as the city and its population continue development.

CHAPTER 6

CONCLUSION AND REFLECTIONS

6.1   Post-Project Observations

The project was officially concluded following the handover of the completed facilities in July 2014. The following section documents observations made from the exchange of correspondence between the two universities and 'review' visits made in the years 2016 and 2017 by the Nanyang Technological University (NTU) team.

6.1.1   Sewage Treatment Plant at the Sri Dalada Maligawa

. . . This plant is very successful. It helps us a lot . . . Especially during crowded days, we have enough problems to remove the wastewater using gully trucks. Municipal Council has only one gully truck. If they are busy, we have to get 4–5 trucks all the way from Colombo. They take 5–6 hours to come here. The whole place is stinking (when the gully trucks come). Now, for the last four years, we only had to call gully trucks twice.

Mr. Lionel Wijesundara, Secretary (International Affairs), Sri Dalada Maligawa

The sewage treatment plant (STP) at the Dalada Maligawa is typically operated at 6.25 m³/day (25% capacity), but can be quickly switched to full capacity of 25 m³/day during peak periods, such as *Poya* day and *Perahara* festival. The plant is managed by a single operator, with the assistance of one to two causal workers on a need basis. A new public toilet for the Dalada Maligawa was built in October 2016 and located close to the wastewater treatment facility and discharges into it. The toilet was built with the support

Fig 6.1 Installation of a public convenience facility within the Dalada Maligawa in 2016.

of the Chinese Government (Fig. 6.1) and has removed the need for the temporary toilets used previously. This has made wastewater management simpler.

The Chinese Government agreed to support the toilet construction because of the (STP) plant.

Mr. W.M.G.A. Bandara, Secretary, Sri Dalada Maligawa

Owing to the proximity of the wastewater treatment plant to the public toilet, visitors have noticed the wastewater treatment plant (there had been no attempt at hiding the facility). As a result, the operator had received enquiry from curious visitors about the plant, and he has been able to explain the treatment plant and how it is operated with some pride.

Sometimes there are universities from England, Australia, India . . . Schoolchildren also come to visit and see the plant. They went to the toilet and happen to see the plant. Sometimes they ask me about the process.

Mr. Senevirathne, STP Technician and Operator, Sri Dalada Maligawa

The facility has been made accessible to the University of Peradeniya (UOP) to assist in its instruction of science and engineering students (Fig. 6.2). Third year undergraduates have modules on conventional and advanced wastewater treatment plants. Postgraduate students are expected

Fig 6.2 University of Peradeniya (UOP) student conducting on site water testing; undergraduates observing wastewater treatment facility at a hotel in Kandy.

to do design work on not only the treatment process, but also the civil and mechanical elements such as the pipelines and pumps. Access to a full-scale operating facility has been useful in providing a case study beyond textbook instruction.

It is a good case study for our students. A lot of details on Kandy Lake and Meda Ela also make good case studies, something people can really see.

Dr. Gemunu Herath, Senior Lecturer, UOP

Our teachers really care about our development.

Ms. Ishanka Wimalaweera, UOP graduate

6.1.2   *Kandy Lake and Mid-Canal Clean-Up*

3–4 months ago (in 2017) catchment management in Kandy came about. Immediate riparian area within 100 m radius from the lake are paid attention to, to identify major and minor source of pollution, including the Kandy General Hospital, and sewerage treatment, oil stations, hotels, restaurants, medical laboratories, garbage disposal . . . We want to streamline all this on top of maintaining of lake and streams (silt management). If we run this catchment management, in two years this effort will be more streamlined.

Mr L.L.A Peiris, Deputy Project Director, Strategic Cities Development Project, Ministry of Megapolis & Western Development

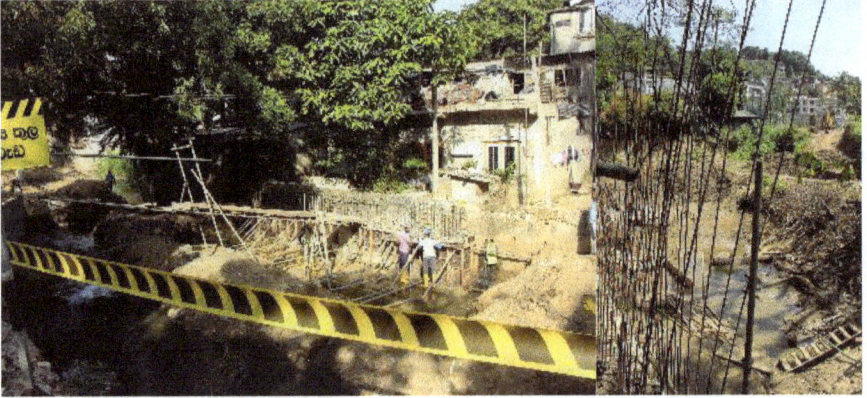

Fig 6.3 Mid-Canal and silt traps.

In 2010, there was still uncertainty if the Kandy city sewerage project will be realised. In 2017, however, construction of Kandy central wastewater treatment plant and its sewer system has been initiated while rehabilitation of silt traps and the Mid-Canal have been on-going. These projects had funding support from the World Bank and the Japan International Cooperation Agency (JICA). Special consideration for Kandy Lake and its environs was made when planning sewer system. Construction of sewer lines and the Kandy Municipal Wastewater Treatment Plant is overseen by the Water Board, and upon completion will be under the Kandy Municipal Council' s management. The Kandy Municipal Council was recognised with the best municipality award, 'the Swarnapura', in 2016 for its services to the public.

New fencing (with low intrusiveness) and signboards were set-up around parts of Kandy Lake (Fig. 6.4), to deter littering and fish feeding. The Irrigation Department also took the initiative to experiment with other colours and species (yellow and pink) of the plant used in the floating wetlands with support from the Peradeniya Botanic Garden and Nuwara Eliya (Fig. 6.5).

There is a start of conversation and discussion among the people in Kandy Lake, more awareness.

Ms. Prabha Dassanayake/ Ms. K.A.D. Kumudini, Engineer, Irrigation
Department, Kandy Region

Fig 6.4 Fencing and signboards newly set up in 2016.

Fig 6.5 New flowers at a makeshift nursery within Irrigation Department's site office, while dredging of sediments at Kandy Lake was on-going in January 2017.

32 projects are on-going, funded by the World Bank. Transport, water, infrastructure . . . 3–4 silt traps are undergoing reconstruction. The World Bank identified the project and had a discussion with everyone . . . The ideas from the (UOP-NTU) project affected decision-making . . . There is much less littering in Kandy now, but still happen especially in slums. Bus terminals are the worst. The municipal council is also including awareness programme for the Meda Ela area.

Mr. Dinuka Senevirathne, Engineer, KMC & UOP Alumni

Following the Kandy Lake project, the NTU, the UOP and the Water Board decided to expand the lake clean-up programme to other lakes in Sri Lanka, starting with Kurunegala Lake in Kurunegala Municipality.

6.1.3   *Education Programme at Mahamaya Girls' College*

It is important to catch the students young to teach them environmental protection and awareness. Such projects introduce students to the world of research before joining the university. Close-proximity to the artificial wetlands model offers an in-house laboratory that has stimulated many students to undertake scientific experiments such as removal of heavy metals by wetland flora.

Mrs. I. Witthanachchi, Principal, Mahamaya Girls College

The model of the wetlands became a valuable teaching opportunity. Samples are collected from the wetland within the school, along with plant species to do other science projects. Some students have presented on related topics and won awards nationally and internationally.

Mrs. Chandrika, Teacher-In-Charge, Mahamaya Girls College

The programme and the club at the Mahamaya Girls' College and the outdoor classroom remain in use and well upkept. Nonetheless the wetland models, because of wear and tear through usage, do need more significant maintenance. Some activities such as events could not be organised more regularly due to limited funds and resources. There is, nevertheless, interest among the teachers and students to use the facility since the school has successfully woven the activities at the outdoor classroom into its core curriculum.

Core school activities that make use of the outdoor classroom include chemistry and biology practicals especially for the advanced level education and this has been arranged to be consistent with the government mandated syllabus. As students learn to practice science skills, such as microscope observation (e.g., for identification of different types of plant tissues), and designing and conducting experiments (e.g., determination of the rate of photosynthesis), having the outdoor classroom helps as a space to conduct and set up experiments and to collect samples. While going outside school premises remains an option for such activities, these often are infrequent because of the need for adequate logistics, supervision and safety considerations when bringing a large number of young students out.

There has been continued connection between UOP and Mahamaya Girls College, in science collaboration, especially with the senior students. Students from the two institutions use the classroom facility for their science projects. These have been pitched at competitions and a number have won awards, such as from the National Science Foundation—thus serving to further highlight the environmental activities championed.

Fig 6.6 The outdoor classroom is in good general upkeep, but wetland tanks need more significant maintenance. Plants around the pond are regularly replaced to introduce different plant species to students.

While the priority in the project was to benefit the public through actual on-ground implementation of technology, the project was conceptualised with the added intention that education (to the partners, community and education institutions) was necessary so as to continue the flow and accumulation of interested and technically competent community members. This is intended to support sustainability of the solutions implemented, so that the local custodians (in this case, the Kandy Irrigation Department and the Sri Dalada Maligawa) would know how to maintain the systems installed after the project has been handed over. Further to this, it is also to build capability and capacity in the community so that as the city evolves, they can innovate and update the systems implemented and so avoid obsolescence and deterioration.

The education component was deliberate and well suited to the two institutions of higher learning, which mandates to train the younger generation and have the infrastructure and the manpower to ensure such training can be accommodated. The project was insistent on documentation of activities therein and this is to facilitate informed copying (versus blind copying of technology, which may result in failure), should

Fig 6.7 Students showing the science awards won by Mahamaya Girls College (MGC), and specimens from their experiment.

the approaches adopted in the project be considered suitable for replication and scale-up elsewhere.

6.2   Reflections on the Lessons Learned and Path Ahead

Urban lakes, like other waterbodies, are often classified based on their geographical and morphological characteristics, but they also have importance attached to them from historical and cultural perspectives. An urban lake is not just a physical body of water but also a socio-cultural complex. As this book has sought to articulate, the acknowledgement of a lake's importance by itself does not directly translate into efforts towards its protection from environmental and human-induced degradation. Efforts that leverage these cultural sensitivities, however, can have the potential to encourage the participation of key stakeholders including citizens for conservation of their environmental resource and heritage (UNEP, 2016).

Taking the socio-cultural and historical context into account while studying the development of an urban lake can provide useful insights into understanding how the lake is valued by the society, the relationship between the city and the lake, an understanding of the changing perceptions of the utility of a lake and the changing ownership and access (Unnikrishnan *et al.,* 2016). There were a number of key issues and opportunities in Kandy project that influenced the design of solutions for lake pollution management. When a lake has high historical and cultural value, the technical aspects of lake management may get side-lined in order to maintain the sanctity of the place. Consequently, the only way out is to design solutions which can accommodate such cultural and social sensitivities.

Das (2015) highlights the 'urban sanitation conundrum' where urban illegal settlements often discharge untreated wastes into surrounding waterbodies. Many of these settlements comprised temporary dwellers without a stable tenure and this discourages any private investment in sanitation and thus, where there is investment, they continue with the most basic levels of sanitation such as septic tanks. Without possibility of connecting to urban sewerage systems, the expectation that urban residents will invest in proper sanitation services is less likely to take effect at any significant scale. The implementation of a wastewater management system had been imperative for Kandy owing to its rising population coupled with a large floating population. Construction of a wastewater treatment plant for Kandy commenced planning on 19 February 2016 with aid from the JICA, and with the Sri Lanka National Water Supply and Drainage Board as the main implementation agency. The sewerage plant when completed is expected to improve water quality at the Mahaweli River. The project aims to provide improved sanitation in the densely populated and low income areas in Kandy, through in-house sanitation facility and refurbishment of public facilities.[1] While launch of the sewerage project is a big step forward in urban sanitation, the current momentum in Kandy Lake pollution management will depend on concerted and continued efforts by all stakeholders.

The Kandy Lake pollution scenario, though having a specific subset of issues unique to it, is also comparable to other urban water pollution scenarios in different parts of the tropical developing world. Therefore, the authors believe the solutions developed for and implemented at Kandy will have general applicability in other tropical developing country contexts as well. The floating wetland system specifically is attractive due to its uncomplicated technology, low capital costs and minimal maintenance requirements. Although, most developing countries are located within tropical and sub-tropical climatic conditions, the adaptation of wetland treatment

---

[1] https://www.jica.go.jp/srilanka/english/office/topics/press160219.html.

technology in these countries has been surprisingly slow and the Kandy Lake project can be a model that can be used to popularise wetland technology in other parts of Sri Lanka as well as in other parts of the tropical developing world. Tropical climatic conditions are conducive to rapid plant growth and hence withdrawal of nutrients from a lake's water. Such conditions support a continuous growing season and higher biological activity can be expected compared to temperate conditions resulting in higher efficiency.

The experience at Kandy Lake has revealed several paradoxes. First, unlike lakes in some parts of the world that are completely neglected because of no seeming utility other than alternate uses of the land the lake occupies for uses such as real estate development, Kandy Lake has high socio-cultural and political significance. Why then did it continue to be polluted? Second, the technical solutions implemented in this case are relatively well established in technical literature, so why was there a need to engage a new project consortium involving international research partners in implementing the same?

Third, policy practitioners in general are known to exercise a great deal of caution in engaging with innovative technological efforts and research ideas that are novel or being implemented for the first time in their jurisdiction. Why in the case of Kandy Lake then were policymakers quite forthcoming in implementing the idea of floating wetlands as well as a new STP, with a technology they are not familiar with, for the Dalada Maligawa?

Upon reflection, some explanations for these paradoxes emerge, which indicate that in cases such as that of Kandy Lake, despite the existence of known technological solutions, political will and mandate for environmental protection, timely application of a 'catalyst' may provide a neutral voice with no local vested interests, give a push to joint action, and help remove bottlenecks to appropriate and concerted action. The catalyst in this case can perhaps be traced to the joint research project and team drawn from UOP and NTU. The role of the catalyst in this case can be seen of as bringing in place, a functional network of stakeholders working together towards the common cause of Kandy Lake pollution mitigation.

While there does not appear to be formal link in the sequence of events that followed the UOP–NTU project, the joint team had managed to articulate the problem and offered a solution. That this solution was sensitive to the lake's context and timing of this solution's articulation was serendipitously consistent with the urgency felt by the Sri Lankans to protect Kandy Lake and its catchment must have helped.

As the authors reflect on the project experience and the subsequent follow-up interviews in Sri Lanka, certain features of this catalyst can be instructive and possibly helpful to identify similar features of potential catalysts elsewhere in Asia for urban lake pollution management:

1. *Being targeted in scope*: While a single project cannot solve the complex problem of lake pollution, breaking it down into clear, sequential and achievable targets however, can help demonstrate to all stakeholders that the issue is not impossible to solve, and consequently revive trust in the authorities and encourage citizen participation in taking care of their environment.

2. *Encouraging citizen education and outreach*: There is a need to move away from blind copying of successful technological solutions elsewhere to informed copying cognizant of the socio-cultural and political context. The local problem also needs to be nested within the larger context. For example, the lake pollution cannot be isolated from the underlying issue of sanitation.

3. *Bringing a 'human dimension' to technical interventions*: Technical solutions for communities and ecosystems need a strong support network and community of people working towards the project's successful implementation and sustenance. This includes both the public at large as well as those operating from the technical side. In this case, it included the team of researchers from both universities as well as the governor. Many of the contractors involved in the Kandy project highlighted that they considered their engagement in the project activities as a service to the temple, and an opportunity to do their part to maintain the Kandy Lake.

4. *Providing an opportunity to innovate by sharing risks*: In such projects, every stakeholder has something at stake, including reputation, financial resources, manpower and time among others. Providing an opportunity to share blame in case things fail can give some degree of security and encouragement to try out new ideas and innovate. In addition, this can also validate ideas through cross-reviews.

5. *Bringing in seed-money to kick start implementation*: Availability of funding in the initial part of project implementation can help fund capital expenses such as the cost of constructing a plant which is often

unavailable given limited budgets of local authorities and multiple pressing priorities. Nonetheless, the existence of such a plant successfully implemented can quickly silence detractors of the larger project.

6. *Demonstrating results at pilot-scale before full-scale implementation*: The project allowed activities to organically develop. For example, the known technology of floating wetlands was first demonstrated at pilot scale in the laboratory before moving on to selected field sites, and thereafter these were installed at all locations identified in the plan.

7. *Engaging practitioners from the initial stage*: The Irrigation Department and Water Board were involved from conception of the idea to the implementation stage. Hence, when it came to handover and continued operations, the transition was easy.

8. *Building a platform for bringing stakeholders together,* and this has to be seen as a neutral enterprise.

9. *Bring in the right mix of people*—the team effort is crucial as there is need to address numerous issues almost simultaneously. Without a team wherein members have common understanding and vision, the effort will become fractured and lose momentum. The project's local champions were very important as ultimate decision-making and ownership must be vested with the local stakeholders. The project had benefited from the close relationships within the original research team which had articulated the idea, and between the universities. This anchored the project.

In closing, extending this research into other cities of historical and cultural significance such as Ho Chi Minh, Siem Reap and Penang is an interesting proposition. It is important to note that many a times some features of this catalyst are present while others are not, and this difference can influence the success of the project. While occurrence of all these features at the same time might be seen as rather difficult or rare to come by automatically, these can be consciously built into the project design right from the inception stage.

REFERENCES

Chapter 1

Anderson, S.C. and Tabb, B.H. (2002). *Water, Leisure and Culture: European Historical Perspectives,* Berg, Oxford, p. 256.

Bai, X., McAllister, R.R.J. Beaty, R.M. *et al.* (2010). Urban Policy and Governance in a Global Environment: Complex Systems, Scale Mismatches and Public Participation, *Cur. Opin. Environ. Sustain.,* 2(3), pp. 129–135.

Department for International Development (DfID). (2010). *Climate Resilient and Sustainable Urban Development.* Printed by The Energy and Resources Institute. Funded by UK Department for *International Development.*

Dinar, A., Seidl, P., Olem, H. *et al.* (1995). Restoring and Protecting the World's Lakes and Reservoirs, Working Papers, World Bank—Technical Papers.

Gunawardhana, M.R., Gunasekara, P.E., Sanjeewani, H.L.G. *et al.* (2009). 'Changing water consumption pattern of Beira Lake and its effects to the city image', in Feyen, J., Shannon, K. and Neville, M. (eds), *Water and Urban Development Paradigms,* Taylor & Francis Group, London.

Henny, C. and Meutia, A.A. (2014). Water Quality and Quantity Issues of Urban lakes in Megacity Jakarta, *LIMNOTEK,* 21(2), pp. 145–156.

Jinadasa, K.B.S.N., Wijewardena, S.K.I., Zhang, D.Q. *et al.* (2012). Socio-Environmental Impact of Water Pollution on the Mid-Canal (Meda Ela), Sri Lanka, *J. Water Res. Prot.,* 4, pp. 451–459.

Kauko, T., Goetgeluk, R. and Priemus, H. (2009). Water in Residential Environments. Climate Change, Flood Risk and Spatial Planning, *Built Environ.,* 35(4), pp. 577–592.

Kora, A.J., Rastogi, L., Kumar, S.J. *et al.* (2017). Physico-Chemical and Bacteriological Screening of Hussain Sagar Lake: An Urban Wetland, *Water Sci.,* 31 pp. 24–33.

Leichenko, R. (2011). Climate Change and Urban Resilience, *Cur. Opin. Environ. Sustain.,* 3(3), pp. 164–168.

Manatunge, J. and Witharana, W.A.U. (2011). 'The tropical environment', in Tanaka, N., Ng, W.J. and Jinadasa, K.B.S.N. (eds), *Wetlands for Tropical Applications: Wastewater Treatment by Constructed Wetlands,* Imperial College Press, London.

Marsalek, J., Jiménez-Cisneros, B.E., Malmquist, P.A. *et al.* (2006). *Urban Water Cycle Processes and Interactions.* IHP-VI—Technical Documents in Hydrology—No. 78 UNESCO, Taylor and Francis Group, Paris.

Mithen, S. (2010). The Domestication of Water: Water Management in the Ancient World and Its Prehistoric Origins in the Jordan Valley, *Phil. Trans. R. Soc. A,* 368 , pp. 5249–5274.

Mowjood, M.I.M. and Sasikala, S. (2011). 'The tropical environment', in Tanaka, N., Ng, W.J. and Jinadasa, K.B.S.N. (eds), *Wetlands for Tropical Applications: Wastewater Treatment by Constructed Wetlands*, Imperial College Press, London.

Nagendra, H. and Ostrom, E. (2014). Applying the Social-Ecological System Framework to the Diagnosis of Urban Lake Commons in Bangalore, India, *Ecol. Soc.*, 19(2), p. 67.

National Water Supply and Drainage Board. (NWSDB). (2016). *Wastewater Management and Kandy City Wastewater Management Project*, S. Godage & Brothers (Pvt.) Ltd., Sri Lanka, p. 172.

Nazul-Islam, M., Kitazawa, D., Runfola, D. *et al.* (2012). Urban Lakes in a Developing Nation: Drivers, States and Impacts of Water Quality and Quantity in Dhaka, Bangladesh, *Lakes Reserv. Res. Manag.*, 17, pp. 253–263.

Rouwendal, J., Levkovich, O. and van Marwijk, R. (2017). Estimating the Value of Proximity to Water, When Ceteris Really Is Paribus, *Real Estate Econ.*, 45, pp. 829–860. doi:10.1111/1540-6229.12143.

Schuler, T. and Simpson, J. (2001). Introduction: Why Urban Lakes Are Different. Urban Lake Management, *Watershed Prot. Tech.*, 3(4), pp. 747–750.

Snehal, P. and Unnati, P. (2012). Challenges Faced and Solutions Towards Conservation of Ecology of Urban Lakes, *Int. J. Sci. Eng. Res.*, 3(10), pp. 170–183

Strang, V. (2012). 'Diverting water: Cultural plurality and public water fatures in an urban environment', in Johnston, B.R., Hiwasaki, L., Klaver, I.J. *et al.* (eds), *Water,Cultural Diversity, and Global Environmental Change: Emerging Trends, Sustainable Futures?* Springer/UNESCO, Paris/Dordrecht/New York. doi:10.1007/978-94-007-1774-9_7.

Strategic Cities Development Project (SCDP). (2014). *Environmental Management & Assessment Framework*, Ministry of Defense and Urban Development. Sri Lanka.

Swedish International Development Cooperation Agency (SIDA). (2007). *Manual for Support to Environmentally Sustainable Urban Development in Developing Countries*. Summary, Draft report, Stockholm.

Tabb, B.H. and Anderson, S.C. (2002). *Water, Leisure and Culture: European Historical Perspectives*, p. 256.

Tanaka, N. and Weragoda, S.K. (2011). 'Wetland plant dynamics. The tropical environment', in Tanaka, N., Ng, W.J. and Jinadasa, K.B.S.N. (eds), *Wetlands for Tropical Applications: Wastewater Treatment by Constructed Wetlands*, Imperial College Press, London.

UNEP. (1994). *UNEP Environment Library No.10—The Pollution of Lakes and Reservoirs*, p. 36.

UNEP. (2000). The Urban Environment: Urban Environmental Management, *UNEP Ind. Environ.*, 23(2), p. 22.

UNEP. (2016). *EnvironmentReligion and Culture in the Context of the 2030 Agenda for Sustainable Development, United Nations Environment Programme*, Nairobi.

UNESCO, Nairobi. (2016). *Culture Urban Future.Global Report on Culture for Sustainable Urban Development*, UNESCO, Paris.

Unnikrishnan, H., Manjunatha, B. and Nagendra, H. (2016). Contested Urban Commons: Mapping the Transition of a Lake to a Sports Stadium in Bangalore, *Int. J. Commons,* 10(1), pp. 265–293. doi:10.18352/ijc.616.

Chapter 2

Abel, P.B. (1989). *Ellis Harwood Series in Wastewater Technology—Water Pollution,* Biology Ellis Harwood Limited, England.
Abeygunawardane, A.W.G.N., Dayawansa, N.D.K. and Pathmarajha, S. (2011). Socioeconomic Implications of Water Pollution in an Urban Environment: A Case Study in Meda Ela Catchment, Kandy, Sri Lanka, *Trop. Agric. Res.,* 22(4), pp. 374–383.
Amarasiri, S. (2015). *Caring for Water.* Greater Kandy Water Supply Project National Water Supply & Drainage Board Pahala Kondadeniya, Katugastota, Sri Lanka. JICA Funded Project.
De Silva, R.K. (1985). *Early Prints of Ceylon (Sri Lanka)1800–1900,* Serendib Publications, London.
Dissanayake, C.B. *et al.* (1982). The Environmental Pollution of Kandy Lake: A Case Study from Sri Lanka, *Environ. Int.,* 7(5), pp. 343–351.
Dissanayake, C.B., Niwas, J.M. and Weerasooriya, S.V.R. (1987, February). Heavy Metal Pollution of the Mid-Canal of Kandy: An Environmental Case Study from Sri Lanka, *Environ. Res.,* 42(1), pp. 24–35.
Hirayama, N. *et al.* (2015). *A Pilot Study of Water Quality and People's Importance Level Towards Sustainable Management of Kandy Lake Basin.* 3rd International Symposium on Advances in Civil and Environmental Engineering Practices for Sustainable Development (ACEPS), January 2015.
Hirayama, N., Honda, R. and Chaminda, T.G. (2016). Factors Affecting People's Preferences on Lake Function for Sustainable Management of Kandy Lake, Sri Lanka.
Jayatissa, L.P., Silva, E.I.L., McElhiney, J. *et al.* (2006). Occurrence of Toxigenic Cyanobacterial Blooms in Freshwaters of Sri Lanka, *Syst. Appl. Microbiol.,* 29(2), pp. 156–164.
Jinadasa, K.B.S.N. *et al.* (2012). Socio-Environmental Impact of Water Pollution on the Mid-Canal (Meda Ela), Sri Lanka, *J. Water Res. Prot.,* 4, pp. 451–459.
Nanayakkara, V. (1971). *A Return to Kandy: Over Balana and Beyond,* Colombo.
Karunarathne, N. (1999). *Kandy Past and Present, Religious and Cultural Fund,* Ministry of Religious and Cultural Affairs, Sri Lanka.
Kawakami, T. Weragoda, S.K., Attanayake, M.A.M.S.L. *et al.* (2011). Fish Die-off and Water Quality in Kandy Lake, a World Heritage Site in Sri Lanka, *J. Ecotechnol. Res.,* 16(2), pp. 39–45.
Knox, R. (1966). *An Historical Relations of Ceylon.*

Strategic Cities Development Project (SCDP). (2014). *Environmental Management & Assessment Framework,* Ministry of Defense and Urban Development, Sri Lanka.

Silva, E.I.L. (2003). Emergence of a Microcystis Bloom in an Urban Water Body, Kandy Lake, Sri Lanka, *Curr. Sci. India,* 85(6), pp. 723–725.

Silva, E.I.L. (2007). Hypertrophic–Eutrophic Alteration in Kandy Lake, Following an Outbreak of a Microcystis Bloom, *Sri Lanka J. Aquat. Sci.,* 12, pp. 115–120.

Chapter 3

Jinadasa, K.B.S.N., Wijewardena, S.K.I., Qing, Z.D. *et al.* (2011). Socio-Environmental Impact of Water Pollution on the Mid-Canal (Meda Ela), Sri Lanka, *J. Water Res. Prot.,* 4, pp. 451–459.

UNESCO. (2016). *Culture Urban Future.Global Report on Culture for Sustainable Urban Development.*

Unnikrishnan, H., Manjunatha, B. and Nagendra, H. (2016). Contested Urban Commons: Mapping the Transition of a Lake to a Sports Stadium in Bangalore, *Int. J. Commons,* 10(1), pp. 265–293. doi:10.18352/ijc.616.

Chapter 4

Dissanayake, C.B., Niwas, J.M. and Weerasooriya, S.V.R. (1987, February). Heavy Metal Pollution of the Mid-Canal of Kandy: An Environmental Case Study from Sri Lanka, *Environ. Res.,* 42(1), pp. 24–35.

Dissanayake, C.B., Senaratne, A., Weerasooriya, S.V.R. *et al.* (1982). The Environmental Pollution of Kandy Lake: A Case Study from Sri Lanka, *Environ. Int.,* 7(5), pp. 343–351.

Guruge, K.S.S., Yamashita, N. and Manage, P.M., (2007). *Mar. Pollut. Bull.* 54, p. 1667.

Jayatissa, L.P., Silva, E.I.L., McElhiney, J. *et al.* (2006). Occurrence of Toxigenic Cyanobacterial Blooms in Freshwaters of Sri Lanka, *Syst. Appl. Microbiol.,* 29(2), pp. 156–164.

Jinadasa, K.B.S.N. *et al.* (2012). Socio-Environmental Impact of Water Pollution on the Mid-Canal (Meda Ela), Sri Lanka, *J. Water Resour. Prot.,* 4, pp. 451–459.

Kandy Municipal Council (KMC). (2000). *Culture Heritage Management and Tourism: Models for Co-operation among Stakeholders,* A Case Study on Kandy, Sri Lanka Submitted to UNESCO, Office of the Regional Advisor for Culture in Asia and the Pacific.

Mowjood, M.I.M. and Sasikala, S. (2011). 'The tropical environment', doi:10.1142/9781848162983_0002, in Tanaka, N., Wun Jern, N.G. and Jinadasa, K.B.S.N. (eds), *Wetlands for Tropical Applications: Wastewater Treatment by Constructed Wetlands,* 1st ed., Imperial College Press, London, pp. 13–28.

National Water Supply and Drainage Board (NWSDB). (2016). *Wastewater Management and Kandy City Wastewater Management Project,* S. Godage & Brothers (Pvt.) Ltd., Sri Lanka.

Pu, J.H., Jinadasa, K.B.S.N., Ng, W. J. et al. (2011). *Numerical Modelling of Kandy Lake, Sri-Lanka in Preparation for Water Quality Improvement.* 6th International Conference on Asian and Pacific Coasts (APAC 2011). December 14–16, 2011. Hong Kong SAR, China, pp. 2050–2056.

Silva, E.I.L. (2003). Emergence of a Microcystis Bloom in an Urban Water Body, Kandy lake, Sri Lanka, *Curr. Sci.*, 85(6), pp. 723–725.

Chapter 5

Kadlec, R.H. and Knight, R.L. (1996). *Treatment Wetlands*, Lewis Publishers, New York.

Pu, J.H., Jinadasa, K.B.S.N., Ng, W.J. et al. (2011). *Numerical Modelling of Kandy Lake, Sri-Lanka in Preparation for Water Quality Improvement.* 6th International Conference on Asian and Pacific Coasts (APAC 2011). December 14–16, 2011. Hong Kong SAR, China, pp. 2050–2056.

Qin, B. (2009, November). Lake Eutrophication: Control Countermeasures and Recycling Exploitation, *Ecol. Eng.*, 35(11), pp. 1569–1573.

Tanner, C.C. (1996). Plants for Constructed Wetland Treatment Systems—A Comparison of the Growth and Nutrient Uptake Characteristics of Eight Emergent Species, *Ecol. Eng.*, 7, pp. 59–83.

UNEP. (2016). *Environment, Religion and Culture in the Context of the 2030 Agendafor Sustainable Development, United Nations Environment Programme,* Nairobi.

Vymazal, J. (2011). Constructed Wetlands for Wastewater Treatment: Five Decades of Experience, *Environ. Sci. Technol.*, 45(1), pp. 61–69.

Wang, G.X., Zhang, L.M., Chua, H. *et al.* (2009, April). A Mosaic Community of Macrophytes for the Ecological Remediation of Eutrophic Shallow Lakes, *Ecol. Eng.*, 35(4), pp. 582–590.

Weragoda, S.K., Jinadasa, K.B.S.N., Zhang, D.-Q., *et al.* (2011). *Tropical Application of Floating Wetlands for Lake Restoration.* Proceedings of the 9th International Symposium on Southeast Asian Water Environment. December 1–3, 2011. Bangkok, Thailand: Vol. 09, pp. 113–120.

Weragoda, S.K, Jinadasa, K.B.S.N., Zhang, D.-Q. *et al.* (2012). Tropical Application of Floating Treatment Wetlands, *Wetlands*, 32, 955–961.

Chapter 6

Das, P. (2015). The Urban Sanitation Conundrum: What Can Community-Managed Programmes in India Unravel? *Environ. Urban.*, 27(2), pp. 505–524.

UNEP. (2016). *Environment, Religion and Culture in the Context of the 2030 Agenda for Sustainable Development, United Nations Environment Programme,* Nairobi.

Unnikrishnan, H., Manjunatha, B. and Nagendra, H. (2016). Contested Urban Commons: Mapping the Transition of a Lake to a Sports Stadium in Bangalore, *Int. J. Commons,* 10(1), pp. 265–293. doi:10.18352/ijc.616.

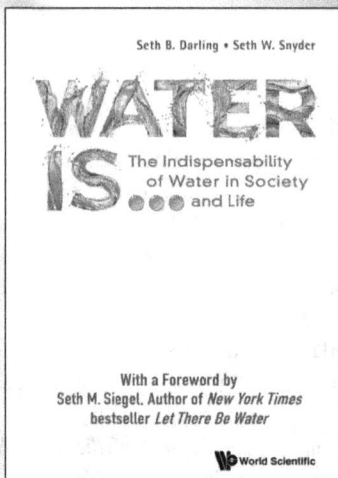

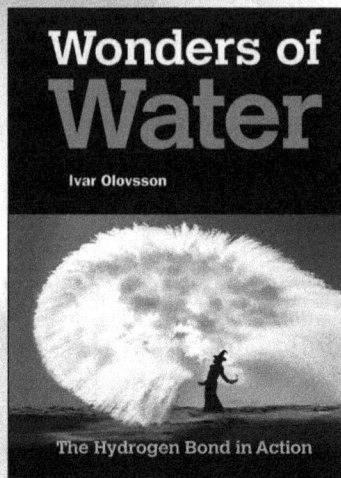

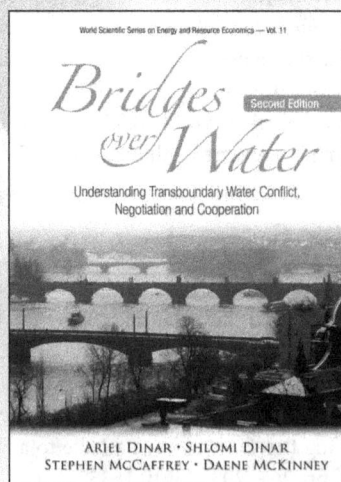